Consequence Management

Operational Principles for
Managing the Consequence
of a Catastrophic Incident
Involving Chemical,
Biological, Radiological,
Nuclear or High Yield
Explosives

CBRNE

Chemical, Biological, Radiological, Nuclear and high-yield Explosive threats

CONSEQUENCE MANAGEMENT: VERSION 1.0

The following is a work-in-progress. Changes will be made. Your input is invited and needed. Please use the evaluation instrument at the end of this workbook to tell us what is good and bad in Version 1.0 and what should be added for Version 1.5. The CBRNE Consequence Management Response Force (CCMRF) is an important new asset. The following attempts to translate existing doctrine, strategy, and lessons-learned to the CCMRF mission. (August 2008)

Consequence Management

Operational Principles for Managing the Consequence of a Catastrophic Incident Involving Chemical, Biological, Radiological, Nuclear or High Yield Explosives

Every effort has been made to ensure the doctrinal, strategic, operational, and tactical accuracy of this publication. It is specifically designed to prepare CCMRF personnel and their civilian counterparts for a sometimes ambiguous and often dynamic mission.

As such it encourages readers to seriously consider how to apply doctrinal and strategic principles to difficult operational and tactical decisions where the correct answer may be less than clear. Any errors are the responsibility of the authors. Please direct concerns regarding accuracy or validity to staff@usarnorth.org.

PURPOSES

1. Familiarize CCMRF battalion and brigade level staff to their mission, roles and responsibilities.
2. Contextualize existing doctrinal guidance to better facilitate effective application of doctrine, strategy, and commander's intent when CCMRF elements face novel problems in the field.
3. Provide senior operational staff with a ready reference to inform decisions during exercises and when deployed.
4. Provide the civilian counterparts of the CCMRF operational staff with information to facilitate their effective collaboration with the CCMRF.

AUDIENCE

CCMRF Commanders and Staff assigned to Task Force Operations, Medical and Aviation and their civilian counterparts.

TOPIC OVERVIEW

TABLE OF CONTENTS

CCMRF

CBRNE Consequence Management Response Force

ABOVE: *Hole in the Pentagon wall following September 11, 2001 terrorist attack.*

CHAPTER 1

CCMRF Mission and Overview

T o assist with a catastrophic mass casualty incident in the United States and its territories — at the direction of the President — the Chairman of the Joint Chiefs of Staff or the appropriate Combatant Commander may deploy the CBRNE Consequence Management Response Force (CCMRF). **The CCMRF is trained and equipped to provide a rapid response capability following a catastrophic event.**

Just as with all instances of Defense Support of Civil Authorities (DSCA), military forces respond only when requested. Requests always work their way up from the local level. After a major incident, city leaders will ask for county assistance; county asks for State assistance; the State Governor asks for Federal assistance from the President. If the President agrees, a Presidential Declaration of Disaster is declared. The Secretaries of Homeland Security, Defense, and other cabinet members meet and determine the best course of action. The SecDef may initiate activation of CCMRF units. State National Guard units are usually mobilized under the direction of the Governor and remain State assets, while CCMRF units are usually Title 10 under the direction of NORTHCOM, ARNORTH, and the Joint Task Force (JTF) Commander — or the Defense Coordinating Officer (DCO) if a JTF is not stood up.

The CCMRF includes assets such as medical surge, chemical decontamination and biological detection that may be helpful to the victims of a catastrophic event. The CCMRF also includes communications, force protection, transportation, supply and maintenance assets that can be used to establish command and control capabilities to facilitate additional military and civilian resources into the affected area.

Joint Doctrine for Civil Support notes, "DOD resources are normally used only when state and local resources are overwhelmed and/or

CBRNE

is an acronym for

**Chemical,
Biological,
Radiological,
Nuclear** and **high-yield
Explosive threats**

Less commonly it also refers to **CBRN**
and **Environmental threats**

It is pronounced **see-burn-ee**.

non-DOD resources of the Federal
government are insufficient or
unable to meet the requirements of
local and state civil authorities."[1]

In this introductory chapter you
will be given a quick overview
of:

- The CCMRF mission in its
  broadest context.
- The practical need for principled innovation and problem
  solving.
- The principled need for operational restraint to preserve
  and support constitutional
  continuity.

---

[1] Joint Chiefs of Staff, **Civil Support,
Joint Publication 3-28**, pages II–1.

2

DEFENDING THE CONSTITUTION

"I ...do solemnly swear (or affirm) that I will support and defend the Constitution of the United States against all enemies, foreign and domestic; that I will bear true faith and allegiance to the same; and that I will obey the orders of the President of the United States and the orders of the officers appointed over me, according to regulations and the Uniform Code of Military Justice. So help me God."**

— (Title 10, US Code; Act of 5 May 1960 replacing the wording first adopted in 1789)

A creative and committed adversary has clearly signaled its interest in securing biological, radiological, and/or nuclear weapons to deploy against the United States. The same adversary has already used chemical and high yield explosive devices against the United States and its allies. CBRNE accidents are also serious.

Much depends on the confidence of the American people.
A poor response will undermine confidence.

Unless quick and effective action is taken, problems can easily spin out of control and undermine public confidence. But **a structured, orderly, courageous, and principled response will enhance public confidence**.

This adversary cannot conquer the United States. Nor can it — directly — threaten the Constitution. But it seeks to use violence and the threat of violence to influence our political process. In October 2003 Osama bin-Laden explained, "I say to the American people we will continue to fight you and continue to conduct martyrdom operations inside and outside the United States until you depart from your oppressive course and abandon your follies and rein in your fools."[2]

---

[2] Al Jazeera.net, October 18, 2003, http://english
.aljazeera.net/English/archive/archive?ArchiveId=40700

DISCIPLINE AND INITIATIVE

In responding to a CBRNE incident **the battlespace and the effects will be among the most complex ever faced**. The battlespace is our own backyard, an American hometown suffering from a catastrophic event.

How the CCMRF combats confusion, fear and anger while cooperating and collaborating with local citizens is a crucial aspect of achieving mission success. The CCMRF will most likely be mobilized under the Civil Support mission of the Department of Defense. (Much more information on the nature of the Civil Support mission will be featured in Chapters III and IV.) Effective coordination with civil authorities will be fundamental to mission success. Local authorities will be in the best position to facilitate the effective application of CCMRF capabilities. The same local authorities will be under enormous emotional and operational stress.

If troops are appropriately trained and exercised to understand the role and limitations of the CCMRF, then their presence and practical assistance can help restore order, confidence, and mutual support. Each Soldier, sailor, airman, or marine can make an important contribution to — or unintentionally undermine — this mission.

The U.S. Army Field Manual No.3-24 (Counterinsurgency) notes, "Successful mission command results from subordinate leaders at all echelons exercising disciplined initiative within the commander's intent to accomplish missions. It requires an environment of trust and mutual understanding. It is the Army's and the Marine Corps' preferred method for commanding and controlling forces during all types of operations."[3]

The Counterinsurgency Field Manual goes on to state, "Young leaders — so-called 'strategic corporals' — often make decisions at the tactical level that have strategic consequences." They must be "trained and

---

[3]   United States Army, **Field Manual Number 3-24**, pages 46–47

educated to adapt to local situations, understand the legal and ethical implications of their actions, and exercise initiative and sound judgment in accordance with their senior commanders' intent."[4]

Counterinsurgency and Consequence Management are very different missions. But they share a common priority to secure the citizens. The more well informed and well-trained strategic corporals, the better.

LEGAL AND OPERATIONAL LIMITATIONS

According to Joint Doctrine, "The Department of Defense provides Civil Support in order to reduce suffering, save lives, prevent or mitigate the destruction of property, manage the consequences of an attack or disaster, or prevent terrorist incidents...The Department of Defense provides Civil Support in order to reduce suffering, save lives, prevent or mitigate the destruction of property, manage the consequences of an attack or disaster, or prevent terrorist incidents by supporting law enforcement."[7] When a CCMRF is deployed to assist with the results of a CBRNE attack or accident, it will do so in support of the civil authorities as specified in the mission assignment (MA) from the Federal Coordinating Officer (FCO) at the Joint Field Office. But there are important limitations on how the military should engage this mission. The limitations reflect core issues of:

1. Competence,
2. Command and Control, and
3. Constitutional Legitimacy.

Competence

As in any mission, there are Lines of Operation (LOs). The CCMRF's primary role in the operation is likely to focus on its specialized competence in biological, chemical, and radiological reconnaissance and decontamination, medical surge, transportation, and communication.

---

[4] Ibid., pages 50–51

After a biological incident, CCMRF may be asked to inspect and test for biological pathogens and toxins such as anthrax; after a chemical incident, CCMRF may detect, analyze and determine what chemical was released; after a radiological incident, CCMRF may perform recon- naissance, using a Chemical Recon Unit to determine the boundries for the primary, fallout and secondary areas and to detect and determine the type of radiation. CCMRF may also perform mass-casualty, life-sav- ing decontamination of civilians and Soldiers. There are other crucial Lines of Operation, but these will most likely be handled by civilian organizations. The Defense Coordinating Officer (DCO) will work with civilian counterparts in the Joint Field Office — the Federal Coordinating Officer (FCO) and State Coordinating Officer (SCO) — as well as local liaison officers (LNO) to determine where and what support is required. The CCMRF unit will not coordinate directly with Civil Authorities, except when actually doing the work per their mis- sion assignment (MA).

Command and Control (C2)

Unity of command is the preferred doctrinal method for ensuring unity of effort by military forces. The nation's Catastrophe Management command structure is organized through the National Response Framework (NRF) and National Incident Management System (NIMS). But unity of command will be important in the immediate aftermath of a CBRNE incident. The civilian communications system is likely to be compromised. A lack of effective civilian command and control may threaten the effectiveness of military C2. Joint Doctrine notes, "A CBRNE event or attack may occur with little or no warning and may overwhelm the response capabilities and resources of local and state jurisdictions…"[5]

It is especially important that dispersed military units maintain regular communications with the military chain of command.

---

[5] Joint Chiefs of Staff, **Joint Doctrine for Civil Support, Joint Publication 3-28**, page III–3

Some Specialized CCMRF Assets

CBIRF IRF Chemical Biological Incident Response Force
(Marines/Navy)

CHEM Co (Decon) Chemical Company Decontamination
(Army)

CHEM Plt (Recon) Chemical Platoon Reconnaissance (Army)

CHEM Plt (BIDS) Chemical Platoon Biological Integrated
Detection System (Army)

NBC Bio Det TM NBC Biological Detection Team (Air Force)

CBRNE CE CBRNE Coordination Element (Army)

HAMMER ACE Hammer Adaptive Communications Element
(Air Force)

AFRAT Air Force Radiological Assessment Team (Air Force)

DTRA CMAT Defense Threat Reduction Agency Consequence
Management Advisory Team (DOD)

ARNORTH, Spokane training

Constitutional Legitimacy

A CCMRF is most likely to be deployed under provisions of the
Stafford Act. According to Joint Doctrine, "A Stafford Act incident is
one in which state and local authorities declare a state of emergency
and request federal assistance. This type of emergency is an incident
for which the Stafford Act established programs and processes for the
Federal government to provide major disaster and emergency assistance to the states, local governments, tribal nations, individuals, and
qualified private nonprofit organizations."[6]

According to the Stafford Act the Federal role in disaster response is to
support the "State and local governments in carrying out their responsibilities to alleviate the suffering and damage...."[7] **The Federal
government does not replace State and local authority or
responsibility.** The Federal government is in a supporting role, not
one of authority or responsibility, to the State and local agencies.
Richard Falkenrath, former White House advisor on Homeland Security
has said, "[T]he basic federal compact... is that the state and local
agencies are responsible for disaster relief and management, and the
federal government is just there to help as asked."[8]

Federal deference to the authority of the fifty-four states and territories
in disaster planning and response has led NORTHCOM officials to note
that no other combatant commander is responsible for maintaining
effective relations with as many sovereign powers.

---

[6] Joint Chiefs of Staff, Joint Doctrine for Civil Support, Joint Publication 3-28, page II-2.
[7] US Government Printing Office, **United States Code Title 42**, Chapter 68, Robert T.
     Stafford Disaster Relief and Emergency Assistance Act, page 1
[8] **Frontline: The Storm**, Interview with Richard Falkenrath, edited transcript available
     at http://www.pbs.org/wgbh/pages/frontline/storm/interviews/falkenrath.html

The Federal government does not replace State and local authority or responsibility.

CBRNE threats

Chemical

Biological

Radiological

Nuclear

High Yield
Explosives

CHAPTER 2
CCMRF Mission Context

This workbook focuses on domestic consequence management under the command of USNORTHCOM.

The CCMRF mission is part of a broader Department of Defense (DOD) support package to the Lead Federal Agency (LFA), which is responsible for overall coordination of the response. The primary agency is responsible for overall coordination of the response. In many cases the primary agency is FEMA, but not always. In the case of many other emergencies the state government retains legal and operational leadership. Often, for these incidents, there is no need to establish a Joint Task Force, and the Defense Coordinating Officer remains the single point of contact for DoD. Other Federal agencies may also support the response — for example, the FBI may assist in collecting evidence — but the primary responsibility remains at the State or local level. There is also likely to be significant involvement in emergency response by local authorities, private organizations, and individual citizens. The legal, political, and operational implications can be complex.

When the CCMRF is deployed, the event has overwhelmed local resources. If the event is perceived as having terrorist origins, the level of public concern will be especially high.

Public concern, legal limitations, and the need to collaborate with a wide range of other players establish a challenging strategic context.

In this chapter you will consider:

- **The Nature of Catastrophe**
- **CBRNE Catastrophes**
- **CM Operational Environment**
- **Major Players in Consequence Management (CM)**

THE NATURE OF CATASTROPHE

When the CCMRF is deployed, someplace in America has almost certainly experienced a catastrophe.

The Catastrophic Incident Annex of the National Response Framework explains, "A catastrophic incident... is any natural or manmade incident, including terrorism, that results in **extraordinary levels of mass**

The response to a catastrophe can be shaped by the type of event it is. For example:

1. The primary agency may differ. For a natural disaster, FEMA is a likely
   primary agency. But for an accidental event, such as a major chemical or nuclear accident, another agency such as the Department of Energy or EPA may be in charge. After an intentional attack, the FBI is likely to be the primary agency.

2. If the effects cross state lines, the response will be more complex. Multiple state emergency operations centers will be established; multiple National Guard commands will respond; and multiple Joint Field Offices may be established. Also, multiple states means multiple political actors: governors, mayors, homeland security directors, etc.

casualties, damage or disruption severely affecting the population, infrastructure, environment, economy, national morale, and/or government functions."

Catastrophes come in three basic types:[1]

Natural catastrophes have their origins in weather events, geological events or the interaction of the two. Examples include hurricanes, tornadoes, flooding, volcanic eruptions, earthquakes, tsunamis, heat emergencies, drought, and wild fires. Biological catastrophes such as the Black Death and the 1918 Spanish Flu Pandemic are less common but have much broader impacts. The CCMRF is made up of units to respond to various degrees of disasters: natural, accidental, and intentional.

Accidental catastrophes are the result of unintentional human error or negligence. Examples include: procedural errors in chemical or nuclear operations, dam failures, truck collisions involving toxic material, train derailments or collisions involving toxic materials, design or engineering failures involving large structures, controlled burns escaping containment, and decisions and non-decisions that increase the vulnerability of large populations in response to an emergency. In the case of an accident on the scale of Chernobyl or Bhopal,[2] a CCMRF deployment is likely.

Chernobyl radioactive contamination area

Power plant at Chernobyl, Ukraine, site of a 1986 radiation release. Background Photo: Wikipedia

Intentional catastrophes are the result of purposeful human decisions to cause death and destruction. Examples include terrorism, warfare, and genocide.

---

[1] This consideration of catastrophe draws heavily on the *Catastrophe Preparation and Prevention* series published by McGraw-Hill Higher Education (2007 and 2008)

[2] Chernobyl, Ukraine is the site of a 1986 release of radiation resulting in many deaths and the evacuation and relocation of 336,000. Bhopal, India is the site of a 1984 release of 40 tons of pesticide killing 3000 to 8000 people.

Death and destruction are common; military personnel know this better than most. But **a catastrophe is a disaster with a scope and scale that implies effective response will be very difficult and full recovery really impossible.**

A catastrophe is an event so disastrous that it changes life as we know it, or how we conduct our lives in the future. The ancient Greek term from which the word is derived means "irreversible change in direction."

A terrorist-spawned CBRNE event will increase public concern about a possible a repeat. An effective, orderly response will help minimize public concern.

How the CCMRF responds to the victims of the attack will save lives and alleviate pain. The CCMRF's mission is to mitigate the catastrophe's footprint: human, geographic, and psychological as much as possible.

CATASTROPHE
an event so disastrous that it
changes everything for always

We certainly must be prepared
to *respond* to catastrophe.
But we never really *recover*
from a true catastrophe.

CBRNE CATASTROPHES

Accident or intention are the most common causes of chemical, biological, radiological, nuclear and high yield explosive incidents.

Each CBRNE agent is unique. One chemical threat is different from another. Biological threats are different from chemical or radiological threats. Even radiological and nuclear events are more different than alike. A CCMRF consists of specialty units focused on selected threats.

Chemical Threats

According to Joint Doctrine for CBRNE Consequence Management (Joint Publication 3-41), "When distinguished by their effects on human physiology, chemical agents fall into five categories: blood (cyanide compounds), blister (vesicants), choking (pulmonary agents), incapacitating, and nerve. Chemical agents can also be categorized by their persistency. Agents are described as persistent when, after release, they remain in the environment for hours to days and non-persistent when they remain for 10 or 15 minutes. Persistent agents are primarily contact hazards while nonpersistent agents are primarily inhalation hazards."

Chemical Incident — Probable DoD Tasks:

- Medical (including "worried well")
- Logistics
- Transportation
- Decontamination

A chemical incident may involve little infrastructure damage. Outside the contaminated area, the communications and healthcare infrastructure will probably be functional, if strained. Most tasks are focused on quickly providing citizens with medical treatment.

"The greatest risk...lies in exposure to inhaled chemicals, but emergency responders may receive lethal or incapacitating dosage through ingestion or absorption through the eyes or skin.

"Regardless of the nature of the toxic chemical, CBRNE Consequence Management will focus on life saving and prevention of further injury tasks to include: responding immediately to treat identified casualties; securing and decontaminating the area to prevent spreading of the chemical; decontaminating people possibly exposed; and providing support to the displaced population." (JP 3-41, page I-5)

Biological Incident — Probable DoD Tasks:

- Medical (including "worried well")
- Logistics
- Transportation

A biological incident may involve very little infrastructure damage; though in a major incident, hospitals may run out of beds. Most tasks are focused on quickly providing citizens with medical treatment.

Biological Threats

According to Joint Doctrine, "Biological agents are divided into two broad categories: pathogens and toxins. Pathogens are infectious organisms that cause disease or illness in their host and include bacteria, viruses, rickettsias, protists, fungi, or prions. Toxins are biologically derived poisonous substances products as by-products of microorganisms, plants, or animals. They can be naturally or synthetically produced."

"Infectious biological organisms represent one of the greatest threats due to their reproductive ability and the time delay from infection to symptom. **An infectious biological attack may remain undetected for several days to weeks after release due to the incubation periods** that biological agents may have. Diagnosis may be slow as many infectious agents have a slow onset and present with nonspecific symptoms that rapidly escalate in severity. Another compounding problem is that patients may simultaneously present in geographically separated areas. Depending on the pathogen, preventive measures and treatment will be difficult to implement due to factors such as large number of casualties, restriction of movement, and quarantine. Finally first responders may be among the first casualties, rapidly overwhelming local and state support systems. Terrorists and other enemy elements may attempt to use biological agents to infect people, agriculture, industry, and the environment." (JP 3-41, page I-7)

Most scientists and public health experts argue that a **pandemic virus** — a new strain of influenza against which humans would have very little immunity — is overdue. Mutations of preexisting viruses occur periodically and unpredictably. A 1918 mutation resulted in 40 to 100 million deaths worldwide. Less deadly mutations were experienced in 1957 and 1968.

Following the invasion of Afghanistan evidence was found suggesting the al-Qaida biological weapons development program was much more advanced than had previously been thought.

In February 2008 the Director of National Intelligence told the Senate Select Committee on Intelligence, "We assess that al-Qaida's Homeland plotting is likely to continue to focus on prominent political, economic, and infrastructure targets designed to produce mass casualties, visually dramatic destruction, significant economic aftershocks, and/or fear among the population. We judge use of a conventional explosive to be the most probable al-Qaida attack scenario...That said, al-Qaida and other terrorist groups are attempting to acquire chemical, biological, radiological, and nuclear weapons and materials (CBRN). We assess al-Qaida will continue to try to acquire and employ these weapons and materials."

Radiological Incident
— **Probable DoD Tasks:**

• Radiological assessment (involves coordination with DOE, NRC, DTRA, National Guard, etc.)
• Decontamination
• Medical (including "worried well")
• Logistics
• Transportation

A radiological incident may be similar in scale to a chemical incident, involving relatively little infrastructure damage. Outside the contaminated area, the communications and healthcare infrastructure will probably be functional, if strained. Most tasks are focused on quickly decontaminating affected citizens and providing medical treatment.

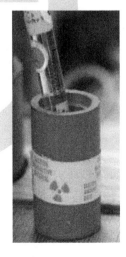

Radiological Threats

Joint Doctrine indicates that the most significant radiologi-cal threat emerges when industrial or medical radioactive materials are weaponized.

"Radiological dispersal devices (RDDs) are devices, other than a nuclear explosive device, designed to disseminate radioactive material in order to cause destruction, damage, area denial, or injury."

"**RDDs are designed to disperse radiation and/or contamination.** One design, called 'dirty bombs,' uses explosives to disperse radioac-tive contamination. A dirty bomb typically generates its immediate casualties from the direct effects of the conventional explosion (i.e. blast injuries and trauma). The main purpose of a dirty bomb is to frighten people by contaminating their environment with radioactive materials and threatening large numbers of people with exposure...."

"By scattering the radiological material, the RDD may create a large area of radiological contamination. The actual dose-rate will be dependent upon the type and quantity of radioactive material spread over the area. This may not be uniformly distributed. As an area denial weapon, **an RDD can generate significant public fear and eco-nomic impact** since the area affected may involve loss of use during a lengthy and costly decontamination process. The contaminated area poses a danger to individuals by external or internal radiological con-tamination. External contamination on individuals can usually be removed by surface cleaning, and by removing contaminated clothing. Internal contamination is much more dangerous and occurs when contaminants are ingested and/or inhaled and concentrate in tissue. This may result in prolonged, high intensity local radiation exposure." (JP 3-41, pages I-8 to I-9)

In 2002 Dr. Henry Kelly, President of the Federation of American Scientists, told the Senate Committee on Foreign Relations, "**Radiological attacks constitute a credible threat.** Radioactive

Nuclear Incident
— Probable DoD Tasks:

• Urban Search & Rescue
• Radiological assessment
  (involves coordination
  with DOE, NRC, DTRA,
  National Guard, etc.)
• Decontamination
• Medical (including
  "worried well")
• Logistics
• Transportation

A nuclear incident is like
combining a massive natu-
ral disaster with a major
health crisis.

There will be massive
structural damage and fire
across a wide area.
Communications and other
critical infrastructure are
sure to be heavily dam-
aged or inoperable. A
range of medical issues
will present themselves,
including burns, radiation
exposure, and trauma suf-
fered in the blast.

materials that could be used for such
attacks are stored in thousands of
facilities around the US, many of
which may not be adequately protected against theft by determined
terrorists. Some of this material could
be easily dispersed in urban areas by
using conventional explosives or by
other methods."

In January 2005 a dirty bomb scare
rattled Boston. The public reaction
was strong enough to cause the
Massachusetts governor to return
from meetings in Washington D.C. In
August 2007 an "unverified radiological threat" resulted in increased law
enforcement activity in New York
City. According to some media
reports, radical websites were pre-
dicting the use of truck bombs to
launch a radiological attack on New
York's financial district.

Nuclear Threats

According to
Joint Doctrine,
"Nuclear detona-
tions cause three
types of injuries: blast, thermal and
radiation."

"Blast injuries are caused by the over-
pressure wave traveling outwards
from the center of the nuclear deto-

20

nation. The types of injuries are the same as occur with conventional explosives."

"Thermal injuries present as flash burns (burns from direct exposure to the thermal radiation pulse, typically ultraviolet, visible, and infrared waves) or flame burns (burns from materials set afire by the infrared energy wave igniting flammable materials.)"

"Radiation injuries from a nuclear blast occur from two sources: prompt and residual. Prompt radiation effects occur due to the neutrons and high-energy gamma rays emitted immediately by the weapon. Severity depends on the weapon's yield, emission spectrum, and distance to the target. Residual radiation effects are due to emissions (typically alphas, betas, and low energy gammas) from fission fragments (the heavy atom products produced during fission and activated environmental materials.... Collectively, these sources are called fallout. The amount of fallout depends on the weapon's yield, type, and height of burst, while the area affected depends heavily on the wind. The hazard to personnel depends on the level of radiation present and the duration of exposure." (JP 3-41, page I-9) The

Explosion of a nuclear weapon at ground level or below will produce more fallout than an air-borne explosion. Depending on the height of the explosion and wind, results can vary significantly.

severity of radiation exposure can be lessened with time, distance and shielding. Limit the time to exposure, put as much distance between you and the radiation, and shield yourself — ideally with lead, but as much as material as possible.

A nuclear explosion releases an **electromagnetic pulse** — an intensely fluctuating magnetic field — which can incapacitate many electrical devices. Depending on the height and yield of the nuclear explosion the pulse can have widespread impact. For example, The Federation of American Scientists has estimated that a high yield nuclear explosion 250 or 300 miles above the Central United States could incapacitate unprotected electronics across the continent.

Joint Doctrine warns, "It is expected that at minimum, local disruptions in information and communications infrastructures will result from EMP. Nuclear detonations may also affect radio transmissions for some hours after the burst." (JP 3-41, page I-10)

In 2005 Senator Richard Lugar of Indiana, then Chairman of the Senate Foreign Relations Committee, surveyed 132 non-proliferation and national security experts. The respondents were asked to assess the likelihood of a nuclear attack anywhere in the world before 2010. The average of all responses indicated a likelihood of 16.4 percent. When asked to assess the likelihood of a nuclear attack by 2015 the average increased to 29.2 percent. The same experts indicated that terrorists are far more likely to launch such an attack (79 percent) than is any nation-state (21 percent).

In June 2006 Mohamed El Baradei, head of the International Atomic Energy Agency, told a Berlin conference, "We worry about sub-national groups, extremist groups acquiring nuclear weapons. It is a nightmare because they will use it."

High Yield Explosives

The most common CBRNE incident involves conventional explosives. Unless the explosion results in the release of dangerous chemicals or radiation it is unlikely the CCMRF will be deployed.

In 1993 a truck bomb using a nitrate with hydrogen gas mixture exploded in the garage below the World Trade Center. The blast was not as effective as the terrorists had planned, but six died and more than 1000 were injured.

The April 1995 attack on the Murrah Federal Building in Oklahoma City also used a truck bomb. One hundred sixty-eight died and 800 were injured.

Improvised Explosive Devices (IEDs) can take many — potentially exotic — forms. The 9/11 attacks used commercial aircraft as guided missiles. The aircraft engine fuel was, in a way, converted into a high-yield explosive. Agricultural chemicals and household chemicals have also been similarly used for lethal purposes.

While federal law enforcement may be involved in response to such events, it would be unusual for military assets to be deployed. **In most cases response to a high-yield explosive accident or attack will be within the capabilities of local emergency responders.**

In 2006 US Army North conducted an exercise that involved terrorist use of three vehicles converted into Improvised Explosive Devices. These weapons were used to target a major football game with 80,000 spectators in attendance.

USARNORTH planning estimated 7062 fatalities and 20,582 injuries. Another 26,400 would present themselves as "worried well." Worried well are just that—healthy people who seek medical attention due to the worry of exposure to an agent or radiation.

In this scenario-based exercise the principal use of military assets related to providing medical surge capacity and mortuary services.

CBRNE and Fear Management

As the USARNORTH scenario suggests, the level of psychological and social impact can amplify the impact of any CBRNE incident.

In the attack excercise on the football game thousands of worried well became a major issue. If the concerns of the worried well can be quickly and credibly resolved, it will be possible to focus more effectively on other priorities.

The USARNORTH exercise identified three objectives:

Assess Incident. Determine the nature of the incident, assess the situation....

Minimize Impact. Implement and coordinate immediate actions to contain the direct effects of an incident....

Care for Public. Implement immediate actions to save lives and meet basic human needs to minimize the impact of an incident and prevent further injury.... (JTF-CS CONPLAN 0500 HYE Playbook, page 9)

A quick and authoritative incident assessment can help to reassure the worried well. In turn, this will enhance the ability of responders to deliver care to the physically injured.

Just as an effective response must address the worried well who are nearby, attention should also be given to addressing the concerns of those at a distance. In responding to any disaster, but especially to a terrorist event, **it is critically important to contain fear**. How to do this will be addressed in considerable detail in chapter 5. But a key to success is for the emergency response to demonstrate — and communicate — competence and confidence.

24

Our own fear is as much an adversary as those who seek to cause fear.

The "worried well" will be a factor in many CBRNE events. With our own human senses, people cannot detect many radiological materials, chemical agents, and biological toxins and pathogens.

Planning for an influx of "worried well" may involve:
- Triage
- Decontamination
- Transportation
- Basic needs (i.e., food, water, shelter, sanitation, etc.)
- Site Security
- Public Affairs (i.e., to deliver accurate information about the real threat to health)

The potential for an influx of "worried well" is a problem that cannot be wished away. It must be planned for.

25

CM OPERATIONAL ENVIRONMENT

A CBRNE catastrophe caused by an accident will present a challenging operational context. If terrorists have deployed a CBRNE weapon the CCMRF will be entering a near "perfect storm" of expectations ranging from the most fundamental human needs to the most extravagant human fears.

According to Joint Doctrine, "During a CBRNE incident, CBRNE Consequence Management efforts must make the preservation of life a priority. This is a significant shift in mind-set for Joint Force Commanders, staff personnel, and CBRNE CM planners." (JP 3-41, page I-4)

The CCMRF's operational context is influenced by both the direct results of the CBRNE event and the legal, political, and social environment.

To confront the realities of catastrophe:

1. Keep in mind your primary mission: To support civilian agencies in saving lives and reducing suffering.

2. Expect the unexpected. In a time of catastrophe, disorder is inevitable.

3. When confronted with chaos...communicate.

4. When *not* confronted with chaos... communicate.

5. Avoid mission creep.

6. Do not exceed your capabilities.

Legal Context

The Tenth Amendment to the Constitution, part of the original Bill of Rights, states, "The powers not delegated to the United States by the Constitution, nor prohibited by it to the States, are reserved to the States respectively, or to the people."

James Madison wrote in Federalist Paper 45, "The powers reserved to the several States will extend to all the objects which, in the ordinary course of affairs, concern the lives, liberties, and properties of the people, and the internal order, improvement, and prosperity of the State."

The States and the people have retained principal responsibility for disaster response, regardless of cause. Federal assistance has remained legally subordinate to state authority.

The current legal framework for federal assistance can be traced to the Disaster Relief Act of 1974. This law established a process for coordinating state and federal relief operations. Federal financial assistance was authorized in case of a Presidential disaster declaration. The scope of potential federal financial assistance was also increased.

On May 6, 1980 President Carter invoked the Disaster Relief Act of 1974 to facilitate federal assistance to thousands of Cuban refugees arriving in South Florida. Under this authority FEMA mobilized military support. Eglin Air Force Base and Ft. Chaffee (Arkansas) were designated as refugee processing centers. Several other military installations would eventually be used. Four hundred Marines were deployed to Key West to assist in maintaining order and processing of refugees. Eventually over 125,000 Cuban refugees would be received in the United States, often at military installations.

In 1988 the **Robert T. Stafford Disaster Relief and Emergency Assistance Act** was adopted. The Stafford Act is designed in part to limit what many saw as a misuse of the Disaster Relief Act of 1974 during the Cuban refugee crisis. The definition of a disaster was considerably tightened and a legal distinction between a disaster and an emergency was created.

27

In many ways, DoD is the responder of last resort. **Before active-duty or reserve military personnel will engage in a domestic response, all of the following have to be unable to cope with the scale of the disaster:**

- Local civilian response agencies
- State civilian response agencies
- National Guard
- Federal civilian response agencies

Shaping the environment for Domestic Support of Civil Authorities (DSCA) means preparing for disasters, but understanding that U.S. military forces will not be used unless absolutely necessary.

The Stafford Act has been amended several times since 1988. Today it is the primary Federal statute giving the President authority to direct federal resources to provide assistance to the states and people.

There are four ways the President may provide support under the Stafford Act:

1. Major Disaster Declaration. The Stafford Act says, "All requests for a declaration by the President that a major disaster exists shall be made by the Governor of the affected State. Such a request shall be based on a finding that the disaster is of such severity and magnitude that effective response is beyond the capabilities of the State and the affected local governments and that Federal assistance is necessary. As part of such request, and as a prerequisite to major disaster assistance under this Act, the Governor shall take appropriate response action under State law and direct execution of the State's emergency plan. The Governor shall furnish information on the nature and amount of State and local resources which have been or will be committed to alleviating the results of the disaster, and shall certify that, for the current disaster, State and local government obligations and expenditures (of which State commitments must be a significant proportion) will comply with all applicable cost-sharing requirements of this Act. Based on the request of a Governor under this section, the President may declare under this Act that a major disaster or emergency exists. (42 U.S.C. 5170, Section 401)

2. Emergency Declaration. The Stafford Act says:

In any major disaster, the President may –

(1) direct any Federal agency, with or without reimbursement, to utilize its authorities and the resources granted to it under Federal law (including personnel, equipment, supplies, facilities, and managerial, technical, and advisory services) in support of State and local assistance response and recovery efforts, including precautionary evacuations;
(2) coordinate all disaster relief assistance (including voluntary assistance) provided by Federal agencies, private organizations, and State and local governments, including precautionary evacuations and recovery;
(3) provide technical and advisory assistance to affected State and local governments for –

(A) the performance of essential community services;
(B) issuance of warnings of risks and hazards;
(C) public health and safety information, including dissemination of such information;
(D) provision of health and safety measures;
(E) management, control, and reduction of immediate threats to public health and safety; and
(F) recovery activities, including disaster impact assessments and planning;

(4) assist State and local governments in the distribution of medicine, food, and other consumable supplies, and emergency assistance; and
(5) provide accelerated Federal assistance and Federal support where necessary to save lives, prevent human suffering, or mitigate severe

Mount St. Helen's erruption, 1980
Source: FEMA.gov

If military personnel are operating under federal authority and in accordance with Title 10 of the U.S. Code, is it is legally permissible for such military personnel to assist law enforcement in executing a search warrant.

☐ Yes

☐ No

☐ It depends

Please explain your answer:

_____
_____
_____
_____
_____
_____
_____
_____
_____

damage, which may be provided in the absence of a specific request and in which case the President

(A) shall, to the fullest extent practicable, promptly notify and coordinate with officials in a State in which such assistance or support is provided; and
(B) shall not, in notifying and coordinating with a State under subparagraph (A), delay or impede the rapid deployment, use, and distribution of critical resources to victims of a major disaster." (42 U.S.C. 5170a, Section 402)

3. Request from a Governor for Department of Defense Support.
The Stafford Act says, "During the immediate aftermath of an incident which may ultimately qualify for assistance under this title or title V of this Act, the Governor of the State in which such incident occurred may request the President to direct the Secretary of Defense to utilize the resources of the Department of Defense for the purpose of performing on public and private lands any emergency work which is made necessary by such incident and which is essential for the preservation of life and property. If the President determines that such work is essential for the preservation of life and property, the President shall grant such

request to the extent the President determines practicable. Such emergency work may only be carried out for a period not to exceed 10 days." (42 U.S.C. 5170b, Section 401)

4. Protecting Federal Facilities. The Stafford Act says, "The President may authorize any Federal agency to repair, reconstruct, restore, or replace any facility owned by the United States and under the jurisdiction of such agency which is damaged or destroyed by any major disaster if he determines that such repair, reconstruction, restoration, or replacement is of such importance and urgency that it cannot reasonably be deferred pending the enactment of specific authorizing legislation or the making of an appropriation for such purposes, or the obtaining of congressional committee approval." (42 U.S.C. 5171, Section 405)

In many emergencies or disasters National Guard units will not be federalized. They will remain under the jurisdiction of Title 32 and the control of their State Governor. As long as National Guard troops are not federalized, they can engage in law enforcement activities that are illegal for federal military personnel.

With a few specific exceptions, federal forces are forbidden from engaging in law enforcement activity by the **Posse Comitatus Act**, now part of Title 18 of the United States Code.[3]

Policy Context

In reaction to the terrorist attacks of September 11, 2001 and the results of Hurricane Katrina (August 2005) the policy environment for disaster response has evolved rapidly. There have been significant changes in how the laws are interpreted and the various roles and responsibilities in disaster relief are conceived.

It is important for military personnel — and their civilian counterparts — to recognize that the policy context is likely to remain fluid for some time.

---

[3] The limitations of the Posse Comitatus Act can be waived, especially when the Insurrection Act is invoked. This will be addressed in chapters 3 and 4.

In working through these issues there are three current expressions of policy that provide important guidance:

1. Homeland Security Presidential Directive 5
2. National Response Framework
3. National Incident Management System

Released in February 2003 **Homeland Security Presidential Directive 5 (HSPD-5)** states in part:

"To prevent, prepare for, respond to, and recover from terrorist attacks, major disasters, and other emergencies, the United States Government shall establish a single, comprehensive approach to domestic incident management. The objective of the United States Government is to **ensure that all levels of government across the Nation have the capability to work efficiently and effectively together**, using a national approach to domestic incident management. In these efforts, with regard to domestic incidents, the United States Government treats crisis management and consequence management as a single, integrated function, rather than as two separate functions...."

In January 2008 a **National Response Framework (NRF)** replaced a previously developed National Response Plan. It states, "Communities, tribes, States, the Federal Government, NGOs, and the private sector should each understand their respective roles and responsibilities, and complement each other in achieving shared goals." (NRF, page 4)

Despite the language of HSPD-5 The National Response Framework is clear regarding a leading role for States and localities. The NRF states, "Even when a community is overwhelmed by an incident, there is still a core, sovereign responsibility to be exercised at this local level, with unique response obligations to coordinate with State, Federal, and private-sector support teams." (NRF, page 5)

The NRF describes the federal role as one of support, "When an incident occurs that exceeds or is anticipated to exceed State, tribal, or local resources, the Federal Government may provide resources and capabilities to support the State response." (NRF, page 6)

To facilitate shared communication and common planning the NRF outlines five principles to guide every level of government and the private sector in a national approach to response:

1. Engaged partnership,
2. Tiered response,
3. Scalable, flexible, and adaptable operational capabilities,
4. Unity of effort through unified command, and
5. Readiness to act. (NRF, page 9)

Of particular importance to the CCMRF's operations is the fourth principle: unity of effort through unified command. This principle is operationalized through the National Incident Management System.

The National Incident Management System (NIMS) is a set of principles and procedures that, if consistently practiced, would improve cooperation and coordination among all those involved in responding to an emergency or disaster.

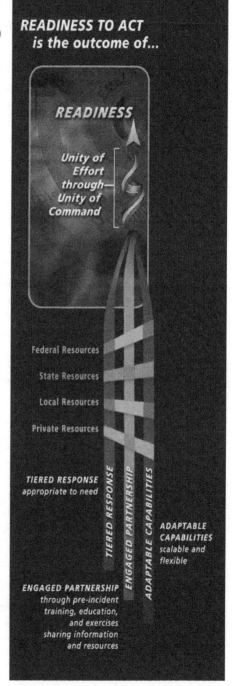

READINESS TO ACT is the outcome of...

READINESS

Unity of Effort through— Unity of Command

Federal Resources

State Resources

Local Resources

Private Resources

TIERED RESPONSE appropriate to need

TIERED RESPONSE

ENGAGED PARTNERSHIP

ADAPTABLE CAPABILITIES

ADAPTABLE CAPABILITIES scalable and flexible

ENGAGED PARTNERSHIP through pre-incident training, education, and exercises sharing information and resources

According to FEMA, **NIMS is a composite of three key organizational systems:**

"The **Incident Command System (ICS)** defines the operating characteristics, management components, and structure of incident management organizations throughout the life cycle of an incident."

"The **Multiagency Coordination System**, which defines the operating characteristics, management components, and organizational structure of supporting entities."

"The **Public Information System**, which includes the processes, procedures, and systems for communicating timely and accurate information to the public during emergency situations." (NIMS Self-Study Guide, page 1-5)

NIMS may best be understood as a set of common management concepts and the beginning of a shared language to allow those involved in prevention, response and recovery to work and communicate across existing professional and jurisdictional boundaries.

Despite the best efforts of NIMS, there is not yet a common language for disaster response. But the language and conceptual descriptions provided by NIMS are a good place to start. NIMS compliance, which includes extensive training, is a prerequisite for participating in several federal funding programs. As a result, the language, principles, and procedures advocated by NIMS should become more common over time.

The Emergency Management Institute, a component agency of the Department of Homeland Security, provides extensive and easily accessible online NIMS orientation and training materials.

Context of Local Capacity

Even in the aftermath of 9/11, a sophisticated terrorist attack that resulted in the largest one-day loss of civilian lives in the nation's history, the City of New York responded with a courage, competence, and capacity that did not require federal intervention. After American Airlines Flight 77 slammed into the Pentagon it was Northern Virginia and District of Columbia firefighters who led the immediate response.

But in each of these cases the physical footprint of the disaster was limited. That will almost certainly not be the case when the CCMRF is deployed.

The worst CBRNE incidents can cause widespread devastation and often involve threat agents for which most localities have little expertise. One of the most difficult issues facing a community in the aftermath of a true catastrophe can be effectively disposing of human remains. This can be a particular problem following a CBRNE incident when remains require decontamination. The ability to carry out this responsibility effectively, safely, and with dignity can contribute substantially to recovery and resilience.

Whatever the local capacity, it is important to take every opportunity to establish effective collaboration and authentic unity of effort. Local emergency responders will always be critically important to understanding the CCMRF's battlespace. The NRF and NIMS provide structures and methods for whatever local expertise is available to be applied, primarily through the Incident Command System.

The CCMRF will remain under military command, but should be familiar with the Incident Command System and coordinate with local resources.

Joint Doctrine emphasizes, "Acts of biological, chemical, radiological, and nuclear terrorism or other catastrophic events represent particular challenges for the traditional ICS structure. Events that are not site specific, and geographically dispersed, or evolve over longer periods of time will require extraordinary coordination between federal, state, local, tribal, private-sector, and Non-Governmental Organizations." (JP 3-28, page D-16)

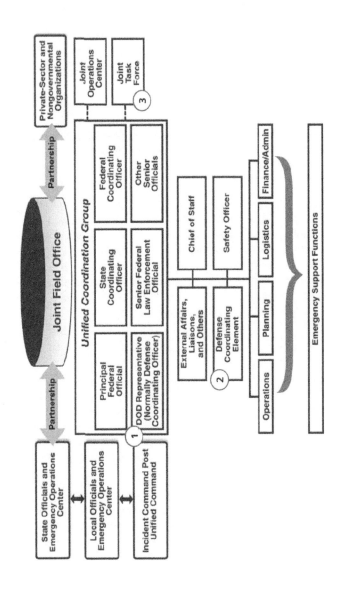

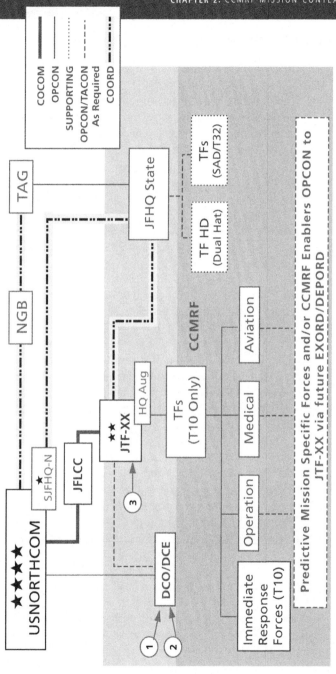

Public Opinion/Political Context

The CCMRF advances its mission by deploying its particular expertise in CBRNE Consequence Management and in providing communications, transportation, medical surge, mortuary surge, and other resources helpful in the aftermath of a disaster.

The CCMRF's **implicit mission** is to support civil authorities in such a manner that a rapid recovery is enabled and public confidence is maintained or restored. The CCMRF — and every element of the civil support function — is focused on reinforcing the resilience of the American people, both those immediately effected by the incident and those outside the disaster zone.

How the CCMRF's mission is achieved and how it is communicated are as important as what is accomplished.

Especially if a CBRNE catastrophe has a terrorist origin **the military mission must include combating fear, confusion, and disorder, including fear and confusion at some distance from the incident.** It is a battle of perceptions. How do the victims perceive the situation? How do those hearing media reports perceive the situation? How does the media perceive the situation?

Joint Doctrine explains, "The public's impression of the assistance depends to a great extent on the media. This perception also influences the cooperation and coordination between military and civilian leaders. Positive public support facilitates mission accomplishment. Lack of public support, on the other hand, can seriously impede the effectiveness of military forces during the execution of CS operations." (JP 3-28, page IV-1)

The Department of Defense Operational Plan for Civil Support (December 2006) states, "The media will play an important role in reporting and shaping public opinion concerning a CBRNE incident and Catastrophe Management response operations. Worldwide media interest in USARNORTH CBRNE operations will be significant and will not be universally favorable…. Any DOD response must take into account possible media repercussions." (JTF-CS OPLAN, page xii)

The OPLAN goes on to say that DOD public affairs "will maintain an active posture throughout CBRNE operations **and work to provide maximum disclosure of timely, truthful information to internal and external audiences.**" (JTF-CS OPLAN, Public Affairs Annex F) Law and policy forbids the use of full-spectrum Psychological Operations during domestic military operations. But Joint Doctrine notes that "DOD may use PSYOP personnel and equipment to support activities such as information dissemination, printing, reproduction, distribution, and broadcasting." (JP 3-41, page viii)

Among the many important tasks of Consequence Management is to respond effectively to the psychological and social dimensions of the crisis. Leadership has sometimes been defined as explaining reality in a hopeful manner. The tough realities should not be obscured. But in responding to disaster the military mission includes forward deployment of every bit of hope that can be mustered.

Read the article on the following page by AP reporter Greg Bluestein.

When the CCMRF is deployed under Title 10 of the US Code it: (Select the correct answer below.)

❑ Is transferred to the command of the State Governor and Adjutant General.

❑ Operates under the command of the Principal Federal Official assigned.

❑ Remains under the command of the President and the Secretary of Defense

The CORRECT ANSWER is "Remains under the command of the President and Secretary of Defense."

MAJOR PLAYERS IN CONSEQUENCE MANAGEMENT

For better *and* worse an effective response to a CBRNE incident will be characterized much more by collaboration than command and control.

The CCMRF will, at all times, remain under the control of the military chain of command and under the direction of the Secretary of Defense and the President. The CCMRF will, however, need to coordinate its activities with a wide range of players.

They include State and local officials, owners and managers of private property, religious and civic organizations, and individual citizens.

"The media will play an important role in reporting and shaping public opinion concerning a CBRNE incident and Catastrophe Management response operations."

Army General Recalls Katrina Aftermath
(excerpted)

By GREG BLUESTEIN The Associated Press
Thursday, September 7, 2006; 4:13 AM

FOREST PARK, GA — When civilian officials couldn't
get a grip on Hurricane Katrina's devastation, it was Lt.
Gen. Russel Honore who took charge, leading federal
troops to help rescue thousands still stranded in New
Orleans days after the storm....

Lt. General Russel Honore
New Orleans, Sept. 21, 2005
Source: FEMA.gov; photo by
Jocelyn Augustino

When Katrina made landfall, the veteran soldier — who once commanded
troops in Korea and prepares troops to deal with explosives in Iraq — approached
the storm as he would a cunning enemy that cut supply lines and communications
with one fell swoop.

Honore soon became an icon of leadership, a walking caricature of a take-
charge soldier whose growling one-liners and commanding presence didn't just
compel his Soldiers into action, but civilians as well....

His mission came with incredible pressure. At stake were the fates of thousands of New Orleans residents and, perhaps, the future role of the military in
domestic disasters.

At its peak, the military's joint task force had 22,000 military personnel, one of
the largest military deployments in the South since troops returned home from the
Civil War. No one knew how the contingent would respond when faced with restive
residents, but many worried it could set a dangerous precedent.

Honore took pains to treat the residents like civilians, not criminals. He
refused to command his troops to forcibly remove the thousands of residents who
refused to evacuate....

The military's response, though, worried some experts who fear local disaster
planners will be more willing to seek federal help instead of preparing a strong,
community reaction.

"I don't ever think we want to be in a place in this country where mayors and
governments aren't in charge," said James Carafano, a homeland security specialist
at the Heritage Foundation. "We don't ever want to be in a place where you transfer
the authority to an unelected official."

Honore defends the military's presence in such an extraordinary situation.

"When the leaders become victims," he said, "the need for outside help was
clearly there."...

41

On the following page is a chart taken from the Army Field Manual for Civil Support Operations. This suggests the complexity of the effort. Yet this chart excludes several important subordinate organizations and does not even try to show relationships with the private sector.

TMI Case Study

Consider the example of what many still consider the most serious potential CBRNE incident in US history. The following is excerpted from a Nuclear Regulatory Fact Sheet on the accident at the Three Mile Island nuclear power plant.

"The accident began about 4:00 a.m. on March 28, 1979, when the plant experienced a failure in the secondary, non-nuclear section of the plant. The main feedwater pumps stopped running… which prevented the steam generators from removing heat.…

"Because adequate cooling was not available, the nuclear fuel over-heated to the point at which the zirconium cladding (the long metal tubes which hold the nuclear fuel pellets) ruptured and the fuel pellets began to melt. It was later found that about one-half of the core melted during the early stages of the accident.

"Although the TMI-2 plant suffered a severe core meltdown, the most dangerous kind of nuclear power accident, it did not produce the worst-case consequences that reactor experts had long feared. In a worst-case accident, the melting of nuclear fuel would lead to a breach of the walls of the containment building and release massive quantities of radiation to the environment. But this did not occur as a result of the Three Mile Island accident."

Local, State, and Federal Disaster Response Coordination (Flood example) — based on the size of a disaster and application of Army, joint, and national doctrine (see chart on right) ⟶

Local and State Disaster Response Headquarters

Federally Managed Disaster

Federal disaster response headquarters and federal military joint task force on site.

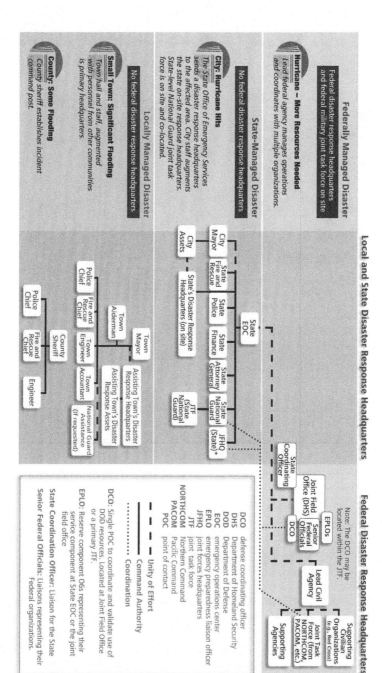

Hurricane – More Resources Needed

Lead federal agency manages operations and coordinates with multiple organizations.

State-Managed Disaster

No federal disaster response headquarters

City: Hurricane Hits

The State Office of Emergency Services sends a disaster response headquarters to the affected area. City staff augments the state on-site response headquarters. State-level National Guard joint task force is on site and co-located.

Locally Managed Disaster

No federal disaster response headquarters

Small Town: Significant Flooding

Town hall and staff, augmented with personnel from other communities is primary headquarters.

County: Some Flooding

County sheriff establishes incident command post.

Federal Disaster Response Headquarters

Note: The DCO may be located within the JTF.

DCO	defense coordinating officer
DHS	Department of Homeland Security
DOD	Department of Defense
EOC	emergency operations center
EPLO	emergency preparedness liaison officer
JFHQ	joint forces headquarters
JTF	joint task force
NORTHCOM	Northern Command
PACOM	Pacific Command
POC	point of contact

— — — Unity of Effort

———— Command Authority

· · · · · · · · Coordination

DCO: Single POC to coordinate and validate use of DOD resources. Located at Joint Field Office or a primary JTF.

EPLO: Reserve component O6s representing their service component at State EOC or the joint field office

State Coordination Officer: Liaison for the State

Senior Federal Officials: Liaisons representing their Federal organizations.

Chart adapted from figure 3-2, page 3-4 of the Army Field Manual for Civil Support Operations

43

In 1979, roughly 25,000 people lived within five miles of the giant cooling towers that became symbols of the nation's worst commercial nuclear accident. Three Mile Island, PA Source: Washington Post, AP photo by Martha Cooper

Even though the actual threat to health was small at Three Mile Island, the incident caused great public concern. **To ensure a coordinated response that can help calm public fears:**

1. Communicate with the chain of command, as well as other responders and civilians as appropriate.

2. If you encounter signs indicating a lack of public confidence in the response, share this information up the chain of command.

3. Achieve your mission objectives. This is the most direct way to improve the situation of those affected.

"The accident caught **federal and state authorities** off-guard.... They did not know that the core had melted, but they immediately took steps to try to gain control of the reactor and ensure adequate cooling to the core. The **NRC's regional office** in King of Prussia, Pennsylvania, was notified at 7:45 a.m. on March 28. By 8:00, **NRC Headquarters** in Washington, D.C. was alerted and the **NRC Ops Center** in Bethesda, Maryland, was activated. The regional office promptly dispatched the first team of inspectors to the site and other agencies, such as the **Department of Energy** and the **Environmental Protection Agency**, also mobilized their response teams."

"Helicopters hired by TMI's owner, **General Public Utilities Nuclear**, and the Department of Energy were sampling radioactivity in the atmosphere above the plant by midday. A team from the **Brookhaven National Laboratory** was also sent to assist in radiation monitoring. At 9:15 a.m., the **White House** was notified and at 11:00 a.m., all non-essential personnel were ordered off the plant's premises. "

"By the evening of March 28, the core appeared to be adequately cooled and the reactor appeared to be stable. But new concerns arose by the morning of Friday, March 30. A significant release of radiation from the plant's auxiliary building, performed to relieve pressure on the primary system and avoid curtailing the flow of coolant to the core, caused a great deal of confusion and consternation. In an atmosphere of growing uncertainty about the condition of the plant, the **governor of Pennsylvania**, Richard L. Thornburgh, consulted with the NRC about evacuating the population near the plant. Eventually, he and NRC Chairman Joseph Hendrie agreed that it would be prudent for those members of society most vulnerable to radiation to evacuate the area. Thornburgh announced that he was advising pregnant women and pre-school-age children within a 5-mile radius of the plant to leave the area."

"Within a short time, the presence of a large hydrogen bubble in the dome of the pressure vessel, the container that holds the reactor core, stirred new worries. The concern was that the hydrogen bubble might burn or even explode and rupture the pressure vessel. In that event, the core would fall into the containment building and perhaps cause a breach of containment. The hydrogen bubble was a source of intense scrutiny and great anxiety, both among government authorities and the population, throughout the day on Saturday, March 31. The crisis ended when experts determined on Sunday, April 1, that the bubble could not burn or explode because of the absence of oxygen in the pressure vessel. Further, by that time, the utility had succeeded in greatly reducing the size of the bubble."

Not referenced above is the involvement of many **county and local leaders** who were instructed by State government to anticipate an emergency evacuation of 650,000 residents. Also left out is the army of news reporters.

Given today's operational context in a similar situation the CCMRF would almost certainly be predeployed to Central Pennsylvania. How do you begin ensuring effective collaboration and unity of effort?

This is a key aspect of shaping and staging and will be addressed in chapter 5.

Emergency Support Functions

In anticipation of, or response to, a major disaster a wide range of
federal, state, and private sector assets will flow toward the affected
region.

The National Response Framework emphasizes the principle of
"engaged partnership." The Army Field Manual for Civil Support
Operations explains, "Engaged partnership begins long before an incident. Leaders of organizations at all levels effectively communicate
shared objectives for planning and operations. They plan together well
in advance of a potential incident so they can cooperate effectively
during a crisis. They ensure all organizations understand one another's
resources and integrate those resources to meet the need. Engaged
partnership includes ongoing communication or actions among all
organizations and shared situational awareness using the NIMS and
NRF terminology and guidance." (Draft FM 3-28, page 2-8)

**The chart to the right identifies a number of the partners with
which you are expected to engage.**

Lessons Learned

In all situations the CCMRF will not be deployed until the bubble has
burst.

Yet as complicated as it is, this situation is familiar to many military
commanders. The need to collaborate with near-strangers is a common feature of counter-insurgency operations. It is a practical challenge for which military personnel have developed tactics, techniques,
and procedures.

"The differing goals and fundamental independence of Non
Governmental Organizations and local organizations usually prevent
formal relationships governed by command authority. In the absence
of such relationships military leaders seek to persuade and influence

46

the 15 Emergency Support Functions

1	ESF 1	Transportation (DOT)
2	ESF 2	Communications (NCS/DHS)
3	ESF 3	Public Works and Engineering DOD (USACE)
4	ESF 4	Firefighting (USDA)
5	ESF 5	Emergency Management DHS (FEMA)
6	ESF 6	Mass Care, Housing (DHS-FEMA)
7	ESF 7	Resource Support (GSA)
8	ESF 8	Public Health and Medical Services (DHHS)
9	ESF 9	Urban Search and Rescue (DHS-FEMA)
10	ESF 10	Oil and Hazardous Materials (EPA)
11	ESF 11	Agriculture and Natural Resources (USDA)
12	ESF 12	Energy (DOE)
13	ESF 13	Public Safety and Security (DHS/DOJ)
14	ESF 14	Long Term Recovery (FEMA)
15	ESF 15	External Affairs (DHS)

DHHS — Dept. of Health and Human Services
DHS   — Department of Homeland Security
DOD   — Department of Defense
DOE   — Department of Energy
DOJ   — Department of Justice
DOT   — Department of Transportation
EPA   — Environmental Protection Agency
ESF   — Emergency Support Functions
FEMA — Federal Emergency Management Agency
USACE — United States Army Corps of Engineers
USDA — United States Department of Agriculture

Integrating Army Operations with National Doctrine

Information Source: Army Field Manual for Civil Support Operations, pg 2-11

other participants to contribute to achieving... objectives. Informal or less authoritative relationships include coordination and liaison.... When unity of command with part or all of the force, including non-military elements is not possible, commanders work to achieve unity of effort through cooperation and coordination among all elements of the force — even those not part of the same command structure."

Here is the briefest possible look at how a mission assignment (MA) comes to DoD:

1. Local and state responders lack the resources to perform a needed task, so they ask federal agencies to assist.

2. A federal Emergency Support Function (ESF) examines its resources. It does not have sufficient capability to assist.

3. The ESF notifies the Federal Coordinating Officer (FCO), who passes a request for assistance to the Defense Coordinating Officer (DCO).

4. The DCO's team analyzes the request and recommends its approval or denial.

5. If the request meets DoD approval, a mission assignment (MA) is created and given to a military unit with the capability of achieving it.

Achieving unity of effort is the goal of command and support relationships.

ARNORTH, Spokane training

*Commanders work to
achieve unity of
effort through*
**cooperation and
coordination**
*among all
elements of
the force.*

CCMRF Guidelines

- Develop measurable objectives

- Coordinate with other organizations

- Plan to hand over tasks

- Provide essential support to the largest number of people

- Know all legal restrictions and rules for the use of force.

US Coast Guard personnel help New Orleans residents to safer areas of the devasted city September 1, 2005 Source USCG photo by PA2 Bobby Nash

CHAPTER 3

CCMRF Operating Procedures and Guidelines

The context in which the CCMRF operates will be difficult — tactically, psychologically, and politically. To negotiate these problems the following principles have been set out:

- **Develop measurable objectives**
- **Coordinate with other organizations**
- **Plan to hand over tasks**
- **Provide essential support to the largest number of people**
- **Know all legal restrictions and rules for the use of force.**
(Draft FM 3-28, pages 1-9–1-10)

The largely unprecedented work of the CCMRF means that many operational variables cannot be fully predicted. As is often the case the CCMRF member will be required to make urgently important decisions under stress.

Awareness of and consistent implementation of the five principles will enhance the ability of the Soldier, airman, sailor, or Marine to advance the CCMRF mission.

When the CCMRF is deployed in response to a disaster there will be an ongoing need for courageous, creative — and principled — decision-making up and down the chain of command. Keeping the chain of command informed is essential. Being prepared to make principled decisions appropriate to purpose and context is a very practical need.

How these five principles are applied depends on the nature of the disaster and the specific situation facing CCMRF personnel. This chapter will give attention to each principle and how the principles are related.

DEVELOP MEASURABLE OBJECTIVES

The Army Field Manual for Civil Support Operations specifies the following measurable objectives:

• **Saving Lives**
• **Protecting Property and Environment**
• **Meeting Basic Human Needs**

In mid-June 2008 many areas of the Midwest United States experienced "500 year floods." Iowa was especially hard hit with over 36,000 long-term evacuations and damage estimates in the billions of dollars. Most of the state was declared a federal disaster area. But the only federal military assets directly involved were Defense Coordinating Officers and a small staff deployed to support FEMA efforts. About 4000 Iowa National Guard personnel were mobilized by the Governor to provide logistical, law enforcement, and emergency coordination support.

June 21, 2008, The Iowa River covered the town of Oakville and surrounding communities with up to ten feet of water.
Source: FEMA.gov, photo by Greg Henshall

In Iowa **effectively focusing on saving lives, protecting property and environment, and meeting basic human needs produced positive results for victims and the military**. What kind of medical care is needed? Where is it needed? By how many is it needed? What is the current capability of non-military medical care? How best can the CCMRF supplement and support existing medical care?

Where is water and food needed? By how many? For how long? What is the local capacity? What is FEMA ready to provide? What are others prepared to provide? How can CCMRF capabilities be best applied to address the need? Which objective will produce the most positive impact? Which objective is the CCMRF most competent to pursue? How can you measure effectiveness? How will you adjust behavior to measures of effectiveness?

The chart below suggests how objectives can be defined, how they can be measured by improved conditions, and how these measurements help advance the desired end-state.

Essential Service Categories and Conditions

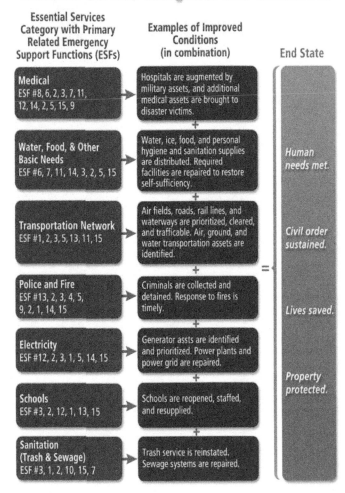

Essential Services Category with Primary Related Emergency Support Functions (ESFs)	Examples of Improved Conditions (in combination)	End State
Medical ESF #8, 6, 2, 3, 7, 11, 12, 14, 2, 5, 15, 9	Hospitals are augmented by military assets, and additional medical assets are brought to disaster victims.	*Human needs met.*
Water, Food, & Other Basic Needs ESF #6, 7, 11, 14, 3, 2, 5, 15	Water, ice, food, and personal hygiene and sanitation supplies are distributed. Required facilities are repaired to restore self-sufficiency.	
Transportation Network ESF #1, 2, 3, 5, 13, 11, 15	Air fields, roads, rail lines, and waterways are prioritized, cleared, and trafficable. Air, ground, and water transportation assets are identified.	*Civil order sustained.*
Police and Fire ESF #13, 2, 3, 4, 5, 9, 2, 1, 14, 15	Criminals are collected and detained. Response to fires is timely.	*Lives saved.*
Electricity ESF #12, 2, 3, 1, 5, 14, 15	Generator assts are identified and prioritized. Power plants and power grid are repaired.	
Schools ESF #3, 2, 12, 1, 13, 15	Schools are reopened, staffed, and resupplied.	*Property protected.*
Sanitation (Trash & Sewage) ESF #3, 1, 2, 10, 15, 7	Trash service is reinstated. Sewage systems are repaired.	

ABOVE: *Adapted from Figure 3-1, page 3-2 of the Army Field Manual for Civil Support Operations. Original chart modified to depict the general relationship between essential services and emergency support functions.*

Meeting Objectives:

1. Other organizations, both civilian and military, will be on the ground, working on the response. Your objectives might be:

    a. In sync with their objectives;
    b. Prerequisite to their objectives;
    c. In conflict with their objectives.

    Be prepared to adapt to shifting circumstances.

2. If the situation on the ground changes, communicate this up the chain of command.

3. If there is anything unclear about your mission assignment (MA) or objective, ask for clarification. Don't make assumptions.

4. When you have met your objective, communicate this up the chain of command and withdraw.

ABOVE: *FEMA Mobile Disaster Recovery Disaster Center (MDRC).* **Right:** *Salvation Army Disaster trailer, set up near FEMA's MDRC, distributes food and drinks to flood victims in Palo, Iowa, June 20, 2008. Source: FEMA.gov, photos by Barry Bahler*

55

Similarity of Chinese, California Fault Systems Raises Concerns *(excerpt)*

By Joel Achenbach
Washington Post Staff Writer
Wednesday, June 11, 2008

Kenneth Hudnut sees trouble out his window. He works in Pasadena, California, in a sunny valley of palm trees, historic bungalows, gourmet coffee shops and elite institutions of higher learning and space technology. But Hudnut, a geophysicist with the U.S. Geological Survey, knows that it also is home to something called the Sierra Madre fault, which is adjacent to something called the Cucamonga fault.

That, in turn, is not far from the fabled San Andreas fault. What worries Hudnut is the possibility of the geological equivalent of dominos: What if an earthquake on one fault causes a chain reaction?

That, he believes, is what happened in China last month in the earthquake that has so far been blamed for more than 69,000 deaths.

"The fault system that ruptured is a lot like the one right out my window here," Hudnut said.

...Hudnut and his colleagues say they believe, based on preliminary data, that at least three different faults ruptured in succession. Rarely has such a cascading event been documented....

James Dolan, a University of Southern California geologist, has put together a map that shows faults in the Los Angeles area butting up against one another like passengers on a subway at rush hour. "Some of these faults could link up in ways we had never anticipated, which could lead to larger events," Dolan said.

LEFT: Cracked pavement on Union Street after the San Francisco earthquake of 1906. Source: California Historical Society, North Baker Research Library

56

COORDINATE WITH OTHER ORGANIZATIONS

To choose meaningful and measurable objectives for the CCMRF you need to know what others engaged in the incident are doing or planning to do. Is the National Guard already on the way to help the police? Is the Coast Guard redeploying to the chemical spills?

The Army Field Manual for Civil Support Operations notes, "When an incident occurs, whether or not advance agreements exist, **coordination with participating organizations must be established quickly and maintained continuously**. Success depends on an agreed upon coordination structure..." (Draft FM 3-28, page 1-9)

Whatever the nature of the emergency — from the incidental to catastrophic — a **Defense Coordinating Officer (DCO)** is assigned. The DCO "serves as the single point of contact at a disaster site for coordinating and validating the use of Federal DOD resources... When a JTF is not required, Title 10 forces are normally placed under operational control of the defense coordinating officer for the response." (Draft FM 3-28, page 2-17)

By actively participating in the Joint Field Office or Joint Task Force established for larger incidents the DCO is usually directly involved in drafting the CCMRF's mission assignment.

The coordination provided by the DCO and staff requires ongoing reinforcement at every level. The Army Field Manual emphasizes, "On-the-ground communication, formal and informal, helps alleviate issues that could delay achieving the end-state. **The coordination and planning occurring in an incident command post, a JFO, and a JTF headquarters may become marginally effective if on-the-ground coordination does not take place.** This is challenging, in part, because organizations have their own cultures and practices. They may interpret the same objectives or directives differently. Soldiers receive their orders in an Army format, but they must be consistent with the overall shared objectives for the response." (Draft FM 3-28, page 3-6)

Coordinating With Other Agencies

During a response, DoD personnel on the ground may be asked to perform additional tasks by civilian responders, outside of their existing mission assignment (MA). When this happens:

1. Analyze the request according to CARRLL factors:

    a. Cost
    b. Appropriateness
    c. Risk
    d. Readiness
    e. Legality
    f. Lethality

2. Get input from your chain of command.

In the case of a CBRNE event, other organizations with expertise similar to the CCMRF are likely to be engaged. These include, but are not limited to:

- Corporate Hazardous Materials Units (e.g. chemical plants, refinery operations, nuclear power stations often have their own response capability)
- Civilian Fire Service Hazardous Materials Units
- National Guard Weapons of Mass Destruction Civil Support Teams (WMD-CST).

These are potentially important sources of information for the CCMRF and assets with which CCMRF capabilities should be tactically coordinated.

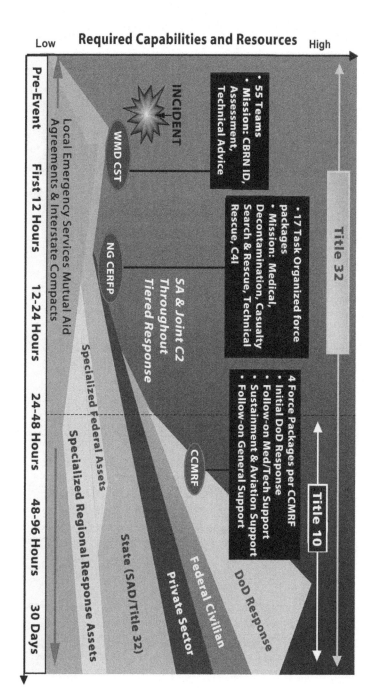

This ongoing process of **vertical and horizontal coordination is essential to effectively targeting all response assets to achieve measurable objectives**. It is especially important to organizing an appropriately tiered response.

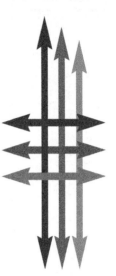

Joint doctrine calls for a "**flexible tiered response.**" This is especially important in terms of a CBRNE incident.

Three tiers are specified in Joint Doctrine for Chemical, Biological, Radiological, Nuclear, and High Yield Explosives Consequence Management:

Tier One is normally implemented for a small scale, localized CBRNE incident... In a Tier One situation, a DCO can effectively exercise command over the small number of DOD forces required and still execute his functional responsibilities with respect to processing mission assignments. An example of a Tier One incident might be a toxic gas release.

Tier Two is the normal response posture for CBRNE incidents having met the Secretary of Defense's criteria to implement CJCS CONPLAN 0500[1] and the need to establish a JTF to respond to the incident. Specialized units, detachments, teams, supplies, and equipment will be required from DOD in the Tier Two response along with enabling and sustainment forces... The commander of a Joint Task Force normally is delegated operational control (OPCON) of all DOD forces... Other JTFs may be established (if required) and referred to as a JTF for consequence management (JTF-CM)." (JP 3-41, page II-22)

A Tier Two response may be engaged before the nature of the incident has been fully determined. Joint Doctrine notes, "CBRNE incidents are difficult for state and local authorities to quickly assess in term of clearly articulating Federal assistance requests and requirements may not be fully appreciated for lack of experience with CBRNE effects. Rather

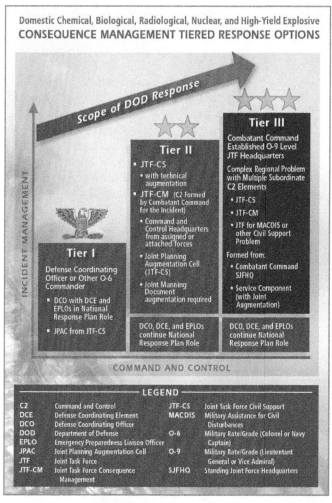

Domestic Chemical, Biological, Radiological, Nuclear, and High-Yield Explosive
CONSEQUENCE MANAGEMENT TIERED RESPONSE OPTIONS

Scope of DOD Response

INCIDENT MANAGEMENT

Tier III

Combatant Command Established O-9 Level JTF Headquarters

Complex Regional Problem with Multiple Subordinate C2 Elements

- JTF-CS
- JTF-CM
- JTF for MACDIS or other Civil Support Problem

Formed from:
- Combatant Command SJFHQ
- Service Component (with Joint Augmentation)

DCO, DCE, and EPLOs continue National Response Plan Role

Tier II

- JTF-CS
  - with technical augmentation
- JTF-CM (C2 Formed by Combatant Command for the Incident)
  - Command and Control Headquarters from assigned or attached forces
  - Joint Planning Augmentation Cell (JTF-CS)
  - Joint Manning Document augmentation required

DCO, DCE, and EPLOs continue National Response Plan Role

Tier I

Defense Coordinating Officer or Other O-6 Commander

- DCO with DCE and EPLOs in National Response Plan Role
- JPAC from JTF-CS

COMMAND AND CONTROL

LEGEND

C2	Command and Control	JTF-CS	Joint Task Force Civil Support
DCE	Defense Coordinating Element	MACDIS	Military Assistance for Civil Disturbances
DCO	Defense Coordinating Officer		
DOD	Department of Defense	O-6	Military Rate/Grade (Colonel or Navy Captain)
EPLO	Emergency Preparedness Liaison Officer		
JPAC	Joint Planning Augmentation Cell	O-9	Military Rate/Grade (Lieutenant General or Vice Admiral)
JTF	Joint Task Force		
JTF-CM	Joint Task Force Consequence Management	SJFHQ	Standing Joint Force Headquarters

Above: *Chart adapted from Figure II-4, page II-23 of the Joint Publication 3-41 (Domestic CBRNE Consequence Management).*

---

[1] Chairman of the Joint Chiefs of Staff Concept Plan 0500: Military Assistance to Domestic Consequence Management Operations in Response to a Chemical, Biological, Radiological, Nuclear, or High-Yield Explosive Situation

than a stable and clearly bounded problem, it will be one of cascading effects and expanding consequences." (JP 3-41, page II-22)

In some instances DoD assets may be staged forward knowing they will called to insure a more immediate response. A common phrase is, "Leaning forward in the foxhole." The Defense Coordinating Officer (DCO), ARNORTH and NORTHCOM will play a part in this decision. In many disasters (such as wildfires, winter storms, flooding, etc.) the DCO, Defense Coordinating Element (DCE), some equipment, and Base Support Installation (BSI) are notified in advance, in anticipation of being asked to support the event. An example of a Tier Two incident might be a small nuclear detonation.

Tier Three involves extremely complex CBRNE scenarios impacting a wide geographic area or a large population or threatening national security. Multiple incidents in different operational areas are supported by multiple JTFs. (JP 3-41, page II-24) An example of a Tier Three incident might be an uncontrollable biological attack

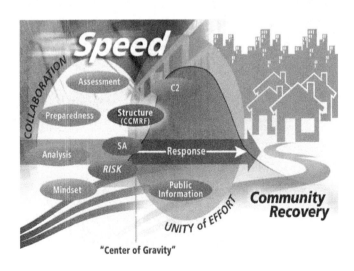

"Center of Gravity"

Wildfires Test
Post-Katrina Emergency Response *(excerpt)*

Spiegel ONLINE, October 24, 2007

Two years on from Hurricane Katrina, everyone has learned a lesson about dealing with natural disasters — not least George W. Bush, who reacted quickly to calls for help.

The largest evacuation in California's history [took place in October 2007] as wildfires rage[d] in the south of the state, with over 500,000 people forced to leave their homes....

Mindful of criticism that the federal government had been slow to respond to Katrina, Bush moved quickly to react to the wildfires. The White House granted California Governor Arnold Schwarzenegger's request for a state of emergency to be declared — which paves the way for federal disaster aid — just one hour after it was received in Washington.... Earlier..., Bush had pro-actively called Schwarzenegger to offer help, rather than waiting for the governor to call him.

By [the next day], the Pentagon had already sent helicopters and troops to California. Homeland Security Secretary Michael Chertoff and David Paulison, head of the Federal Emergency Management Agency, were also on their way....

Los Angeles County fire battalion chief Arthur Ellis told the Wall Street Journal that improved communication with other state and federal agencies, such as the US Forest Service, had allowed him to better coordinate fire-fighting efforts.

Swift emergency response efforts are thought to have contributed to the low death toll so far....

PLAN TO HAND OVER TASKS

One of the benefits of close coordination is that this becomes a strong foundation to hand over tasks once the CCMRF's role begins to wind down.

The Army Field Manual is clear that the CCMRF should "hand over disaster response...to civil organizations as soon as feasible. **The time to plan for the handover is at the beginning of the civil support operation.** The timing and feasibility of the transition is linked to collectively establishing, measuring, and achieving... the end-state of the overall incident response effort."

"Army leaders continually assess the objectives of civil leadership and the communities they assist. They cooperate and follow coordination procedures all organizations understand, consistent with the NIMS and NRF. Once Army actions are completed civil organizations take over the response effort. Army forces normally complete their tasks before the NIMS-based end state is reached; this is as it should be. **Transferring tasks to civil authorities and withdrawing Army forces are positive signals to the citizens being supported.** They indicate that the community has recovered enough for civil authority to assume operations, life is returning to normal, and Army forces have successfully completed their support mission. (Draft FM 3-28, page 1-9)

Planning the hand-over will be an example of the sort of iterative design that is also used in Counter Insurgency operations.

Iterative design consists of:

- **Assessment and Problem-setting**
- **Commander's Visualization**
- **Critical Discussion and Coordination**
- **Systems Thinking**
- **Continuous Assessment** [2]

It can be difficult to establish a common operating picture of a disaster. Especially in the aftermath of a CBRNE event misinformation and lack of information will be common.

Iterative design differs from traditional planning in its tentative and open engagement of the problem. Traditional planning focuses on solving a well-defined problem. Iterative design is concerned with problem-setting in a highly ambiguous context.

When situations do not conform to established frames of reference — when the hardest part of the problem is figuring out what the problem is — planning alone is inadequate and iterative design becomes essential.

Commanders begin developing their design upon receipt of a mission. Design precedes and forms the foundation for staff planning. However, commanders continuously test and refine their design to ensure the relevance of action to the situation.

Critical to the Commander's Visualization of the problem is

---

[2] These elements of Iterative Design draw heavily on similar guidance provided in the Counterinsurgency Field Manual (FM 3-24). See Chapter 4 of the COIN Manual.

ABOVE: June 25, 2008, trucks carry debris from flood damaged Cedar Rapids, IA. Source: FEMA.gov, photo by Greg Henshall

Plans apply established procedures to solve a well-defined and largely understood problem.

Iterative design operates within a highly ambiguous context to conceive a framework for solving complex problems.

communication among the commander, principal planners, local authorities, state and federal officials, and interaction on the ground. The object of this dialog is to achieve a level of situational understanding at which the approach to the problem's solution becomes clear. As a result, design focuses on framing the problem rather than developing courses of action. (FM 3-24, pages 139-141)

According to the Army Field Manual, this process is built into the National Incident Management System (NIMS). The Army Field Manual for Civil Support Operations says, "The NIMS communications and information management component... includes guidance for overcoming the challenges of sharing information in a multiple-organization environment."

The NIMS emphasizes that the common operating picture is formed through "gathering, collating, synthesizing, and disseminating information." The Army Field Manual warns, "This NIMS concept is slightly different from the Army term common operational picture, defined as a single display of relevant information within a commander's area of interest tailored to the user's requirements and based on common data and information shared by more than one command." (Draft FM 3-28, page 2-7)

For example, if provision of clean water is identified as a key problem-to-be-solved, action may depend on availability of electricity, which may depend on availability of fuel, which may depend on availability of transport, which may depend on the availability and willingness of transport drivers.

Fog and friction complicate military operations in response to disaster just as is the case in wartime.

Clausewitz famously wrote that a commander "is constantly bombarded by reports both true and false; by errors arising from fear or negligence or hastiness; by disobedience born of right or wrong interpretations, of ill will, of a proper or mistaken sense of duty, of laziness, or of exhaustion; and by accidents that nobody could have foreseen." He might have been writing of consequence management. (*On War*, page 193)

By working with others to set the problem and establish measurable objectives to realistically engage the problem, the CCMRF can contribute substantially to the desired end-state of restoring civil capacity for response and recovery.

PROVIDE ESSENTIAL SUPPORT TO THE LARGEST NUMBER OF PEOPLE

In a military response to a CBRNE event the "enemy" includes immediate pain and suffering, prospective pain and suffering, confusion, uncertainty, and fear.

In a combat situation it is common to calibrate decisions with:

- **Mission**
- **Enemy**
- **Terrain and weather**
- **Troops and support available**
- **Time available**
- **Civil Considerations**

Sometimes abbreviated as **METT-TC**, these decision factors also apply to Consequence Management. Given the situation and your resources, how can the CCMRF best advance the mission and vanquish the enemy?

The Army Field Manual for Civil Support Operations notes, "...leaders constantly assess requirements so they can determine optimal use of finite military resources. Based on common objectives and in coordination with other supporting organizations, they assign resources. To help assess requirements, leaders use military intelligence resources to gain information. For example, unmanned aircraft systems (UAS) can help survey routes and locate displaced citizens. Army civil affairs or dedicated disaster assessment teams, combined with other civilian assets such as the Civil Air Patrol, may be leveraged to collect information needed for decisions concerning resource allocations. Combining traditional and non-traditional means of collecting and processing information helps leaders adjust resource allocations." (Draft FM 3-28, page 1-10)

In the case of several CBRNE threats time may be an especially complicating factor.

This operational principle is closely related to the main target of the CCMRF mission. JTF-CS OPLAN 005 is very clear, "The Strategic Center of Gravity (COG) is public trust. The decisive points to protect this Center of Gravity are the media and public confidence, and USNORTHCOM's timely execution of its Strategic Communications Plan in coordination with the Lead Federal Agency." (JTF-CS OPLAN 0500, page 7)

By delivering against the measurable objectives, doing so in a way that clearly serves the largest number of people, and effectively communicating this mission outcome, the CCMRF makes a crucial contribution to the maintenance of public trust in the military, in civilian authority, and in the Constitution.

Photo Source: Corbis Royalty Free Collection 248

The Strategic
Center of Gravity
is public trust.

Comparative Orders of Battle
for a Catastrophic Event

Uncertainty

Confusion

Death

Destruction

Fear

Public
Trust
Essential Services
Restored
Effective
Communications
Health Care
Courage &
Competence
Threat Clarification
Strategic Centers
of Gravity

KNOW ALL LEGAL RESTRICTIONS AND RULES FOR THE USE OF FORCE

The military commitment to preserve and protect the Constitution includes abiding by federal, state, and local laws developed under the Constitution. This is especially important in conducting domestic operations.

National Guard personnel may, depending on State laws and the direction of the chain of command, directly support law enforcement and are sometimes specifically trained to exercise police powers. But this is only the case when they continue to operate in a State Active Duty (SAD) status, as Title 32 or non-federal troops.

Military personnel involved in civil support operations should be briefed on and demonstrate familiarity with the Standing Rules for the Use of Force for US Forces (see Appendix).

According to Joint Doctrine, "Under imminently serious conditions, when time does not permit approval from higher headquarters, any local military commander, or responsible officials of other DOD components may, subject to any supplemental direction provided by higher headquarters, and in response to a request from civil authorities, provide **immediate response to save lives, prevent human suffering, or mitigate great property damage**." (JP 3-28, page II-6)

"This participation should be of short duration, lasting only until sufficient local and state assets arrive on the scene and assume control. Consequently, immediate response authority is not a blanket authority to provide unlimited military assistance any time and any where for any length of time." (JP 3-28, page II-8)

In *Wayne v United States* (1963) Judge Burger wrote for the majority:

"...The need to protect or preserve life or avoid serious injury is justification for what would be otherwise illegal absent an exigency or emergency.... A myriad of circumstances could fall within the terms 'exigent circumstances'... e.g., smoke coming out a window or under

a door, the sound of gunfire in a house, threats from the inside to shoot through the door at police, reasonable grounds to believe an injured or seriously ill person is being held within." (Wayne v. United States, 318 F.2d 205, 212 (D.C. Cir. 1963))

Other Principles

The Army Manual for Civil Support Operations articulates two other key operational principles:

Treat all civilians encountered as US citizens — All Soldiers, Sailors, Marines, Airmen, leaders, staff, civilians, and contractors, treat all civilians encountered as US citizens who deserve the best care possible. Members of the Armed Forces strive to treat everyone with dignity and respect. The carrying of weapons during a Defense Support of Civil Authorities (DSCA) or CBRNE-CM mission can be authorized only by the Secretary of Defense.

Commanders at all levels are responsible for training their personnel to understand and properly utilize the SRUF.

Joint Publication 3-28 Civil Support

ABOVE: National Operations Center
Source: US Department of Homeland Security (DHS.gov)

Terminology and Language

Military personnel involved in Civil Support Operations are expected to be fluent in the terminology used by the Department of Defense and the language used by civilians involved in emergency operations.

The Army Field Manual for Civil Support Operations notes, "All organizations participating in incident management and response, including Army forces, are directed to use these NIMS and NRF procedures and terms." (Draft FM 3-28, page 2-2)

As an example, the Army Field Manual offers the following, "NIMS and NRF... do not include the idea of giving and receiving orders as in a purely military environment. A designated civilian incident commander could be said to give "orders" to subordinates within his or her chain of authority. But for the most part, this commander directs other organizations. The civilian use of command, in a cooperative environment, means that tasks are carried out by groups and individuals who agree to perform them. In a cooperative environment, organizational relationships are not purely hierarchical. Therefore Army leaders adapt their leadership style not only to cooperate with other groups but also to encourage cooperation among all participating organizations and individuals. Army leaders keep in mind that they serve in a supporting role." (Draft FM 3-28, page 2-4)

Military personnel are encouraged to become fully familiar with the concepts and terminology the National Response Framework, the National Incident Management System, and other common tools of civilian emergency response. According to the Army Field Manual for Civil Support Operations it is the obligation of military personnel to adapt their processes to what civilians will readily understand. "Army leaders, staff, and Soldiers communicate planned Army actions to other organizations using formats and technology understandable to those organizations."(Draft FM 3-28, page I-9)

During the Reconstruction period immediately following the Civil War the War Department was charged with law enforcement in the occupied former Confederacy. Young army officers were assigned to the Bureau of Refugees, Freedmen, and Abandoned Lands, commonly called the "**Freedmen's Bureau**," charged with keeping the peace and solving problems associated with the end of slavery. The involvement of federal troops in law enforcement and related activities during the Reconstruction era led to the passage of the **Posse Comitatus Act** and the broad prohibition regarding United States military involvement in law enforcement.

CHAPTER 4

CCMRF Roles
and Organizational Structure

The CBRNE Consequence Management Response Force (CCMRF) is a ready asset for responding to a catastrophic event. The CCMRF has expertise in responding when chemical, biological, radiological, nuclear, or high-yield explosive threats are involved. But the CCMRF may also be used for rapid-response when other threats have overwhelmed local resources and a Department of Defense Civil Support mission has been authorized.

The prior chapters have outlined the CCMRF's mission context — a catastrophic event — and the legal, strategic, and operational principles that should guide mission execution. This chapter will focus on the assets available to the CCMRF, the role of the CCMRF, and how the CCMRF is related to other key resources involved in consequence management.

When the State and local capacity to respond has been overwhelmed the CCMRF and other federal resources are used as a surged response to stabilize local conditions and to provide an opportunity for local authorities to recover their capacity.

Some of this surge capacity is specialized. The CCMRF has CBRNE detection and decontamination expertise that may not exist locally. But the CCMRF also has communications, transportation, medical, and other resources that can be helpful in a wide array of disaster response operations.

How CCMRF resources are effectively integrated into the overall response will have a considerable influence on unity of effort and achievement of mission. The Department of Defense is committed to a flexible response. As a result, the specific assets available to a particular CCMRF will — to the extent possible — be tailored to the needs of the catastrophic event.

The CCMRF's role and relationships will also be flexible. Awareness of planning assumptions and basic expectations will support the flexibility.

This chapter will address:

• CCMRF Capabilities
• Command and Control Relationships
• Roles and Responsibilities

CCMRF CAPABILITIES

Current plans are for three CCMRFs of roughly 4500 personnel each. CCMRF-1 is ready. CCMRF-2 is expected to be deployable in 2010 with the third CCMRF standing up in 2011.

For planning purposes each brigade-strength CCMRF includes at least **three task forces: medical, aviation, and operational.** The operational assets include transportation, communications, logistics, public affairs, psychological operations and intelligence as well as specialized CBRNE detection and decontamination units.

For planning purposes **each brigade-strength CCMRF includes at least** **three task forces:**

Operational | Aviation | Medical

The **CBRNE specialty units** are likely to be assigned to the CCMRF on an as-needed basis depending on whether the threat is chemical, biological, radiological, nuclear or high-yield explosives. According to JTF-CS OPLAN 0500, "The CBRNE-CM mission will be accomplished using: (1) designated CBRNE-CM response forces; or (2) regionalized response forces identified and sourced at execution; or a combination of both." (JTF-CS OPLAN 0500, pages 22-23)

An Army chemical brigade is the likely source for many functional spe-cialities. The brigade is comprised of five conventional and specialized chemical battalions. There will eventually be 29 subordinate companies stationed throughout the country. Which company or companies are assigned to the CCMRF will depend on the nature and location of the disaster.

Other potential sources for functional expertise include United States Marine Corps Chemical-Biological Incident Response Force [USMC CBIRF], the National Guard [State JTF headquarters], WMD Civil Support Teams [CST] and CBRNE Enhanced Response Force Package [CERFP]. Other than the CBIRF, these forces are not Title 10 forces.

The CBRNE units are likely to use either the M93 Fox Reconnaissance Vehicle or the next generation Nuclear Biological Chemical Reconnaissance Vehicle (NBCRV). Both of these units can detect contamination in the immediate environment without exposing the crew.

Decontamination will often be achieved through use of the Modular Decontamination System (MDS). This consists of a decontaminant pumper module to mechanically dispense and brush or scrub DS2 and other field decontaminants on victims and vehicles. DS2 is a non-aque-ous liquid composed of 70% diethylenetriamine, 28% ethylene glycol monomethyl ether, and 2% sodium hydroxide. This has been found effective for a wide variety of contaminants. With a high-pressure washer, an MDS provides the Soldier an improved capability to perform decontamination with reduced water usage, labor, and processing time.

In the aftermath of a CBRNE event — or any catastrophic event — the CCMRF's transportation, logistics, communications and other opera-tional assets can also contribute to achieving several response missions.

In current plans, up to four Infantry Battalions are assigned to the CCMRF. The personnel, trucks and other transportation assets of these battalions can provide crucial support in case of mass evacuation, delivery of urgent food, water, and medical supplies, or mortuary services.

If the disaster has compromised the commercial communications infrastructure the CCMRF's own communications systems may be essential to incident command and unity of effort. By the time actual Consequence Management Operations begin, JTF-CS OPLAN 0500 calls for "establishment of the communications architecture to include connectivity between USARNORTH, DOD forces, local first responders, Lead Federal Agencies, CCMRF Task Forces and subordinate task elements." (JTF-CS OPLAN 0500, page K-8)

A typical **Task Force Aviation** for the CCMRF will consist of a:

• Headquarters, Aviation Brigade
• Aviation Battalion Medical Lift
• Aviation Battalion Medical
• AVIM (maintenance and supply) Platoon (JTF-CS OPLAN 0500, page A-3)

Equipment typically available to aviation units includes heavy and medium lift helicopters (CH-47D, E, F, and others). Most Army Aviation Branch companies will deploy with 8 to 16 personnel/cargo lifting helicopters, capable of carrying 33 to 44 individuals or 24 litters plus two medical attendants. UH-60 Blackhawk helicopters are also commonly used as air ambulances capable of carrying a flight crew, six litters, and one medic.

While the Aviation Task Force is configured primarily for medical support, JTF-CS OPLAN 0500 identifies other possible uses, including transportation, evacuation, airspace command and control, and general aviation support. (JTF-CS OPLAN 0500, page 32)

JTF-CS OPLAN 0500 identifies **seven priorities for Task Force Medical:**

- Provide public health support,
- Provide medical augmentation to existing hospitals or other medical facilities,
- Provide definitive medical care,
- Establish casualty collection points/emergency medical care locations,
- Assist with patient movement (air/ground),
- Provide medical logistics support,
- Support patient redistribution through National Disaster Medical System (NDMS).

A Level III facility provides both intensive and resuscitative care and is staffed by 200 health care professionals. A Level III facility is essentially a small hospital with the capacity for surgery, emergency medicine, critical nursing care, internal medicine, OB/GYN, radiology, pulmonary medicine, anesthesia, nutrition, community health and mental health.

A Level II medical facility is typically staffed by fewer than 50 health care professionals and focuses mostly on treatment and release or condition stabilization for transport to a Level III or more advanced facility.

Other medical resources likely to be made available by Task Force Medical include a Theater Epidemiological Team, a Biological Assessment Team, Blood Program Unit, Force Health Protection Unit, and a Veterinary Services unit.

The force package will be tailored to specific need. But as an example of the capacity possible, JTF-CS OPLAN 0500 has outlined a possible time-phased deployment as shown on the following page.

ABOVE: *The Boeing Chinook 47-D can perform multiple roles*

NOTIONAL

1 The first deployments assess and secure the area of operations and/or respond to the most urgent needs:

- Joint Task Force-Civil Support Headquarters
- Personnel Detachment
- Movement Control Team (MCT)
- Chemical/Biological Incident Response Force (CBIRF)
- HAMMER Adaptive Communications Element (ACE)
- Support Headquarters Advanced Echelon (ADVON)
- Aviation Headquarters Advanced Echelon (ADVON)
- Defense Threat Reduction Agency (DTRA) Consequence Management Advisory Team (CMAT)
- CBRNE Civil Engineering (CE) detachment

2 The second force package delivers core services, including expanded communications and the full set of field and clinical medical care. These elements include:

- JTF-CS (Follow-on)
- Headquarters and Headquarters Detachment Support Brigade
- Expeditionary Medical Support Units
- EPI TM
- 2 Medical Companies
- Special Medical Augmentation Response Team (SMART)—Electronic Medical Records
- SMART—Nuclear, Biological, Chemical
- Defense Logistics Agency (DLA) Contingency Support Team (CST)
- ACCE
- Aviation Battalion
- Aeromedical Evacuation Liaison Team
- Digital Topography team (DIGI TOPO)
- Force Provider Company (FP CO)
- Headquarters and Headquarters Detachment Support Battalion
- Signal Company
- Headquarters and Headquarters Detachment Support (Medical) Battalion
- Brigade Combat Team HG C2
- Air Force Reserve Ammunition Team (AFRAT)
- Military Public Affairs Detachment
- Chemical Company (Decontamination)
- Chemical Platoon (Reconnaissance)
- Aviation Headquarters
- SMART—Health System
- SMART—Pastoral Care
- SMART—Stress Management
- 2 HAMMER ACE
- Navy Meteorology and Oceanography Detachment (METOC)
- CAISE Advance Echelon (CAISE ADVON)

3 The third force package deployment

reinforces those units already in the area of operations and begins to introduce recovery and transition resources:

- Headquarters and Headquarters Company, Medical Brigade
- Medical Detachment (Sanitation)
- Brigade Operational Law Team (BOLT)
- Force Provider Company
- Nuclear Biological Chemical — Biological Detection Team
- Medical Logistics Unit
- 3 Medical Strike Teams
- Quartermaster Supply Company
- Engineering Support Unit
- Mortuary Affairs Team
- Aviation Maintenance Unit
- Transportation Unit
- Headquarters, Communications Specialist Company
- 2 Communications Companies
- CAISE
- Aviation Medical Battalion
- Headquarters, Force Provider Battalion
- Headquarters and Headquarters Detachment, Area Support Brigade

This phased deployment includes a wide array of moving parts. Despite training and exercising, many of these units will not have previously deployed together. The operational environment of the CCMRF will be chaotic and, if anything, domestic deployment can be more complicated than operating outside the United States. The **effective calibration of the parts depends on Unified Action** by all military components and unity of effort between military and civilian components.

1st force package

*operations area
urgent needs*

2nd force package

core services

3rd force package

*reinforcement
recovery and
transition*

Both joint and service doctrines emphasize the preeminent need for Unified Action. The Army Field Manual for Operations explains, "Unified action describes the wide scope of actions (including the synchronization of activities with governmental and nongovernmental agencies) taking place within unified commands, subordinate unified (subunified) commands, or joint task forces under the overall direction of the commanders of those commands. Public law charges combatant commanders with employing military forces through unified action. Under unified action, commanders integrate joint, single-service, special, and supporting operations with interagency, nongovernmental, and multinational...operations." (FM 3.0, section 2-1)

Unified Action by the CCMRF depends on several preconditions.

• **First**, each component part must be at the highest possible stage of functional readiness to perform their particular role with competence and full capacity.

• **Second**, each military unit must give careful consideration to its Operations Orders (OPORD) and consider how the OPORD fits within the principles and strategy.

• **Third**, operations must be combined with ongoing and purposeful communications. The following guidance relates to Civil Support Operations as much as warfighting: "Operational commanders continually communicate with their strategic superiors to obtain direction and ensure common understanding of events. Mutual confidence and communications among commanders and staffs allow the flexibility to adapt to tactical circumstances as they develop." (FM 3.0, section 2.8)

Be ready, think deeply about your role in advancing the overall mission, and communicate constantly.

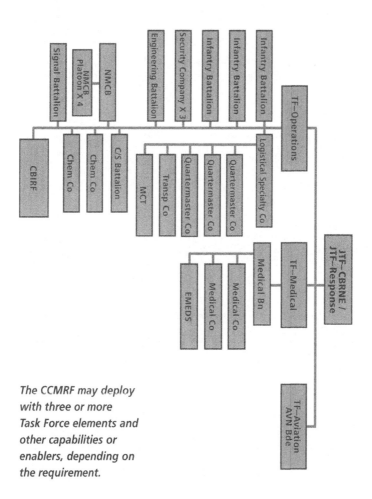

The CCMRF may deploy with three or more Task Force elements and other capabilities or enablers, depending on the requirement.

COMMAND AND CONTROL

C ommand and Control of the CCMRF is straightforward and consistent with other military missions. The need to coordinate military command and control with non-military incident management adds complexity.

In response to a Presidential Declaration and authorization the Secretary of Defense designates a Combatant Command to respond. For most domestic disasters USNORTHCOM will be the choice. Acting on behalf of the Secretary, the Joint Director of Military Support (JDOMS) will cut an Execute Order (EXORD) to delineate support relationships, available forces, end-state, purpose and approved scope of actions. (JP 3-28, page II-18). Depending on the nature of the disaster and the EXORD the Combatant Command may designate a Joint Task Force-Civil Support to undertake the mission.

The JTF-CS Commander will dispatch a NORTHCOM Situational Awareness Team (NSAT) to the disaster area to determine the scope and magnitude of the CBRNE event. The NSAT findings will determine whether the CCMRF receives an actual deployment order (DEPORD) and Mission Assignments.

The EXORD, Operations Order (OPORD), DEPORD, and Mission Assignments (MA) all provide important guidance in terms of how **the CCMRF contributes to the strategic end-state and mission through Unified Action** and facilitates Unity of Effort with non-military partners.

The CCMRF will usually deploy to support a wide variety of civilian agencies that are outside the military command and control system, each of which have very different approaches to C2, and — because they are working their way through a local disaster — are operating at less than their own top strength. Yet the mission is to support — not replace — local leadership.

What Are Your Orders?

OPERATIONS ORDER (OPORD) — Narrative-Task Organization

1. ( ) SITUATION

    (1) ( ) Enemy Forces

    (2) ( ) Friendly Forces

    (3) ( ) Attachments and
        Detachments

2. ( ) MISSION

3. ( ) EXECUTION

    (1) ( ) Concept of Operations

    (2) ( ) First Tasking Assignment

    (3) ( ) Second Tasking Assignment

    (4) ( ) Remaining Tasking Assignment(s)

    (5) ( ) Coordinating Instructions

4. ( ) ADMINISTRATION & LOGISTICS

5. ( ) COMMAND AND SIGNAL

Preserve or restore public trust by
- Saving Lives
- Protecting Property and Environment.
- Meeting Basic Human Needs

National Guard, local police, local firefighters, local health care professionals, NGOs, who or what else?

Who, what, when, where, how, and why?

Fear, confusion, uncertainty? Weather conditions and terrain?

What is the status of civilian communications?

Depending on the nature of the disaster, what does the combination and sequence of tasking assignments suggest regarding the Commander's visualization and Commander's intent?

How will you coordinate with local authorities?

What are your resources for achieving mission and tasking?

87

Unity of Effort is the term used to describe the relationship between military C2 and the incident command system specified by the National Response Framework (NRF) and National Incident Management System (NIMS). The Army Field Manual for Civil Support Operations explains Unity of Effort as the outcome of unified command:

> The NIMS term "unified command" refers to the teamwork and management coordination among representatives of multiple commands (and jurisdictions), both civilian and miltary, toward common objectives. Unified Command is based on the Incident Command System (ICS) and is used for complex, multi-jurisdictional incidents (rather than a single incident commander). Unified Command requires that each participating organization understand the roles and responsiblities of the others. A lead civilian agency directs the overall disaster response effort, and participating organizations, including Army forces, jointly manage that effort to meet overall objectives. (Draft FM 3-28, page 2-8)

The CCMRF is most likely to contribute to unity of effort when its **operations are coordinated through the incident command system and at the direction of the Joint Field Office (JFO)**. Incident command is more focused on tactical response while the JFO is more oriented to strategic outcomes.

"The **Incident Command System** defines the operating characteristics, interactive management components, and structure of incident management and emergency response organizations engaged throughout the life cycle of an incident. Direct tactical and operational responsibility for conducing incident management rests with the incident commander. The incident command structure develops in a top-down, modular fasion that is based on the size and complexity of the incident, as well as the specifics of the hazard environment created by the incident. The ICS organization has five major functions. These are: command, operations, planning, logistics, and finance and administration." (JP 3-28, page D-16)

At the lowest tactical level the Incident Command System is represented by an Incident Command Post (ICP). An ICP can be anything from a single police officer using his cruiser radio and a cell phone to a more capable mobile and multifunctional ICP similar to a military Forward Command Post.

"The **Joint Field Office** is a temporary federal facility established locally to provide a central point for coordinating federal, state, local, and tribal rsponse to the incident..." The JFO provides "strategic leadership and coordination for the overall incident management effort, as designated by the Secretary of Homeland Security. The JFO organizational structure is built upon the National Incident Management System (NIMS) but does not impede, supersede, or impact the ICP/ICS command structure." (JP 3-28, page D-18)

On the following page is a graphic representation of the National Incident Management System (NIMS) framework taken from Joint Doctrine for Civil Support. For the purposes of this graphic the CCMRF is one of the Task Forces at the bottom. Command and Control remains with the JTF commander, a two-star or three-star general officer. The JTF commander and

Achieving Unity of Effort

1. Other organizations contribute to mission success.
   a. Local first-responders and governmental agencies
   b. Local businesses
   c. State assets
   d. Federal civilian assets

2. Politics plays a part.

3. Societal stability and order are key objectives.

Implications for CCMRF Forces

1. Be on the lookout for potential conflicts between your mission and others' missions. Communicate these up the chain-of-command. Both military commanders and civilian coordinating officers need to be aware of such conflicts.

2. Know your authority under Immediate Response, as well as your limitations under Posse Comitatus. Achieve mission success without overstepping your bounds.

3. Civilian responders can be a valuable source of information. Communicate this up the chain of command.

staff interact regularly with the Defense Coordinating Officer (DCO) and staff assigned to the Joint Field Office. **The DCO has significant influence to ensure strategic coordination of military assets** to achieve the end-state communicated by the Principal Federal Official (PFO) or Federal Coordinating Officer (FCO).

Also notice the **coordination line between subordinate components of the Joint Task Force, such as the CCMRF, and an Incident Command Post.** How this coordination is achieved is one of the most important factors in achieving mission success. It has not been common, but it is possible for the JTF to have a dual status commander. This allows the same individual to command both Title 10 and Title 32 forces, as well as National Guard troops on State Active Duty (SAD) status. For this to happen the President and the State Governor must agree on the same National Guard commander, who already has Title 32 authority, to be federalized and assume Title 10 authority reporting to the Combatant Commander. It is also possible for an active duty officer to be appointed by the Governor, with the consent of the President, to command National Guard forces.

The benefit of a dual status commander is to allow Title 32 (National Guard) forces to retain their more flexible roles and responsibilites yet advance unity of effort through unity of command.

The dual status commander does not change the legal status of Title 32 or Title 10 forces under his or her command. The legal limitations on Title 10 forces are preserved, as are the legal and operational distinctions between federal and state forces. The Army Field Manual for Civil Support explains. "A dual status commander serves as the link for two separate chains of command." (Draft FM 3-28, page 1-8)

A recurring issue in Consequence Management — as in most military missions — is how to ensure tactical engagements advance strategic success.

There are two ways the military can support civil authorities. The first is in response to a formal tasking communicated through the military chain-of-command. Military personnel can also engage in "immediate response" to a local request or emerging situation. There are times when the formal tasking and the need for an immediate response can seem in tension or even in conflict. How is the tension or conflict resolved?

The first and best solution is to communicate the situation up the chain-of-command. But there are times when communications are compromised or the need for immediate response is so urgent that lives will be endangered by the time taken to communicate. **When it is not possible to resolve a potential conflict by communicating with higher command, the Soldier must make a decision** based on his or her understanding of the mission, the Commander's visualization, Commander's intent, and the principles set out in strategy and doctrine.

The strategies and principles set out in the prior chapters might be summarized as follows: **In Civil Support Operations in order to secure the Strategic Center of Gravity (Public Trust) the military will consistently act to provide essential support for the largest number of people.**

CCMRF ROLES AND RESPONSIBILITIES

The nature of the disaster will have a significant impact on the specific roles and responsibilities assigned to the CCMRF and its Task Forces.

In the case of most domestic disasters the Department of Homeland Security, usually operating through FEMA, will generate mission assignments. The Joint Task Force-Civil Support will treat these mission assignments as Requests For Assistance (RFAs). For the military chain-of-command the RFA's "become mission assignments only after they have been approved by the Secretary of Defense.... The Commander-Joint Task Force will exercise Operational Control (OPCON) and Tactical Control (TACON) over all designated DOD forces as directed by the

Command and Control Relationships

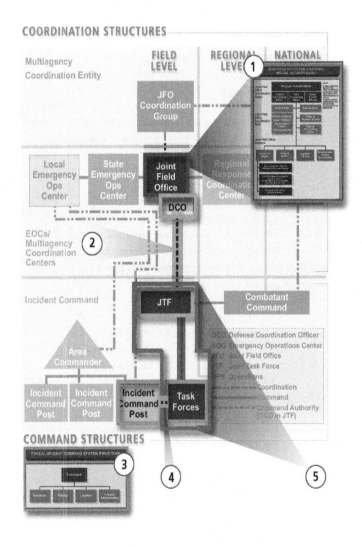

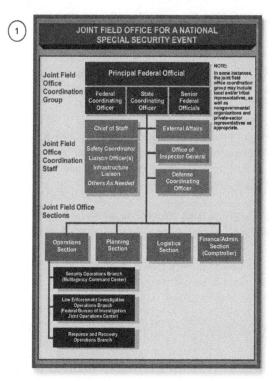

① **JOINT FIELD OFFICE FOR A NATIONAL SPECIAL SECURITY EVENT**

② The JTF Commander and staff interact regularly with the Defense Coordinating Officer (DCO) and staff assigned to the Joint Field Office.

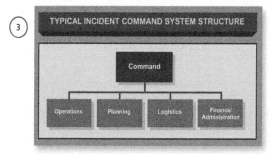

③ **TYPICAL INCIDENT COMMAND SYSTEM STRUCTURE**

④ Notice the coordination line between subordinate components of the Joint Task Force, such as the CCMRF, and an Incident Command Post. How this coordination is achieved is one of the most important factors in achieving mission.

⑤ Command and Control remains with the JTF Commander. (Structure assumes CCMRF as a Task Force)

Combatant Commander's EXORD. The JTF may task organize function-ally, by Service components, or a combination of both, depending on the situation." (JP 3-41, page II-29)

The chart below is taken from Joint Doctrine for Chemical, Biological, Radiological, Nuclear and High-Yield Exposives Consquence Management. It highlights some of the most common roles and responsibilites that may be assigned to the CCMRF.

Specific taskings will come in the form of Mission Assignments (MA's), originating from the Joint Field Office.

To speed the development of MA's, several have been pre-scripted, though not pre-approved. For military purposes they remain RFAs until approval by the Secretary of Defense or designate has been validated.

ANTICIPATED TASKS AND REQUIREMENTS

Joint Task Force Headquarters provides command and control, and coordination for the following types of tasks and requirements through functional task forces

Incident Site Support	Medical Support	Logistic Support	Headquarters Support
• Coordination with Local Emergency Management Director	• Triage/Treatment	• General Support Logistics	• Communications
• Facility Decontamination	• Definitive Care	• Joint Reception, Staging, Onward Movement, and Integration	• Technical Augmentation
• Surveying, Monitoring, and Marking of Incident Site	• Medical Logistics		♦ Intelligence
• Site Management	• Hospital Augmentation	• Displaced Population	♦ Mapping
• Command and Control of Area Support	• Epidemiological Support	• Mortuary Affairs	♦ Modeling
• Critical Skills Augmentation	• Agent Technical Support	• Transportation	♦ Weather
	• Stress Management	• Rotary-Wing Aviation	• Public Affairs
	• Preventative Medicine		
	• Veterinary Support		
	• Prophylaxis/ Immunization		
	• Patient Decontamination		

ABOVE: Adapted from Figure 11-7, page II-29, Joint Publication 3-41 Chemical, Biological, Radiological, Nuclear, and High-Yield Explosives Consequence Management (02 October 2006)

Transitioning to civilian authority is the final mission objective.

ABOVE: *Navy divers from Mobile Diving and Salvage Unit (MDSU) 2 from Naval Amphibious Base Little Creek, VA, prepare to enter the water at the site of the I-35 bridge collapse over the Mississippi river at Minneapolis. MDSU-2 is assisting other federal, state, and local authorities managing disaster and recovery efforts at the site. USNORTHCOM is responsible for coordination of all active-duty military forces serving in Defense Support of Civil Authority roles.*
Source: northcom.mil, photo by Seaman Joshua Adam Nuzzo.

CHAPTER 5

CCMRF Operations

There are five phases of Civil Support Operations:

- Phase I: Shaping
- Phase II: Staging
- Phase III: Deployment
- Phase IV: Civil Support Operations
- Phase V: Transition

Each phase is critically important.

The CCMRF may be involved in multiphase operations.
Depending on the nature of the disaster the CCMRF could be engaging Phase V in one community while in another jurisdiction Phase III is still underway. It is also possible that in the same area of operations a particular CCMRF function — such as CBRNE detection — will be completed while another — such as Task Force Medical — is still staging.

A principal benefit of this **phased approach** is to emphasize the extensive preparation needed for tactical operations to be successful. The CCMRF cannot suddenly be configured and deployed and reasonably hope to achieve its mission.

Another benefit of phasing is to remember — and to help others recognize — that transitioning to civilian authority is the final mission objective.

PHASE I: SHAPING

Familiarize yourself with:

- **Civilian disaster response mechanisms**
  - Read the National Response Framework, especially the Catastrophic Incident Supplement.
  - Take online NIMS course(s) from FEMA

- **Military command and control structure for the response to a domestic incident**
  - Participate in online and classroom-based courses from ARNORTH
  - Read JTF-CS OPLAN 0500
  - Read Joint Publication 3-41, "Chemical, Biological, Radiological, Nuclear, and High-Yield Explosives Consequence Management."

- **Military personnel tasked with domestic incident response. For example:**
  - Defense Coordinating Officers/Elements (DCO/Es) in each FEMA Region
  - National Guard WMD-Civil Support Teams (WMD-CSTs)
  - National Guard CBRNE Enhanced Response Force Packages (CERFPs)

- **Indications and warnings of future threats**
  - Track open sources on chemical, biological, radiological, nuclear, and IED threats

- **Likely CCMRF taskings and responsibilities in the event of a CBRNE incident**

Phase I: SHAPING

According to JTF-CS OPLAN 0500, "Phase I is continuous situational awareness and preparedness and monitoring indications and warnings (I&W). Actions in this phase include inter-agency coordination, exercises, and public affairs outreach (which continues through all phases). Main effort during this is Joint Task Force-Civil Support. The phase ends with identification of a potential CBRNE-CM incident." (OPLAN O500, page ix)

The problem in consequence management is being bombarded by so many new and unexpected problems that the mind can not make sense of the flood of events and experiences. Situational Awareness reduces this problem by familiarizing the human mind with a range of possible problems in advance, exposing how the problem components are related, and exploring potential solution paths.

Some of the elements important to the CCMRF are observed patterns of catastrophic events — and especially CBRNE events — anywhere in the world. By familiarizing CCMRF personnel with these past and unfolding events they will be better prepared to confront their future challenges.

A critical step is thinking through the problems experienced in the examples. What patterns are exposed? What relationships are exposed? What strategies were effective? Which strategies failed? Given the lessons-learned, what are the most important decision-points? What are the most important tasks?

Traditional indications and warnings are events or actions that suggest an enemy attack may be near or is already underway. Unfortunately, CBRNE threats seldom come with such undeniable warning signals.

During the Shaping Phase the CCMRF will find it helpful to establish relationships with civilian agencies such as regional Terrorism Early Warning (TEW) groups. By working with civilian organizations it is more likely the CCMRF will develop a Common Operating Picture similar to the civilian authorities the CCMRF will be supporting when deployed. This information can also contribute to the work of the J2 intelligence function. One of the principal J2 products is the Consequence Management Area Assessment. According to JTF-CS OPLAN 0500 the "CM Area Assessments provide baseline information on critical infrastructure, terrain, and population densities." (JTF-CS OPLAN 0500, page B-3)

The best Shaping activity is often a realistic tabletop or field exercise involving the full range of first responders confronting an overwhelming problem-set. **Successful exercises stress the system enough to cause failure.** Learning from fictional failure is the best way to prepare for real success.

Phase 1: **SHAPING**

Continuous situational awareness
  and preparedness

Monitoring indications and warnings

Actions
• **inter-agency coordination**
• **exercises**
• **public affairs outreach**

Main Effort
• **Joint Task Force–Civil Support**

Phase 1 ends with
• **identification of a potential**
  CBRNE-CM incident

Shaping
for a Dirty Bomb Attack

- What do you know about a dirty bomb?

- What do others in your unit know about a dirty bomb?

- How well prepared are civil authorities to deal with the consequences of a dirty bomb?

- What would your unit's likely role be in a CCMRF response to a dirty bomb explosion?

From the Council on Foreign Relations:

What is a "dirty bomb"?

A "dirty bomb," also known as a radiological weapon or a radiological dispersal device (RDD), is a conventional explosive packaged with radioactive materials. A dirty bomb kills or injures through the initial blast of the conventional explosive, and by airborne radiation and contamination (hence the term "dirty").

How much expertise does it take to make a dirty bomb?

Not much more than it takes to make a conventional bomb. No special assembly is required; the regular explosive simply disperses the radioactive material packed into the bomb. The hardest part is acquiring the radioactive material, not building the bomb.

Even so, expertise matters. Not all dirty bombs are equally dangerous: the cruder the weapon, the less damage it causes. It is unclear whether terrorists have access to the sophisticated technologies needed to work with high-grade radioactive material.

Which radioactive materials could be used to make a dirty bomb?

Many types of radioactive materials with military, industrial, or medical applications could be used in a dirty bomb. Weapons-grade plutonium or freshly spent nuclear fuel would be the most deadly, but these are also the most difficult to obtain and handle. Medical supplies such as radium or certain cesium isotopes used in cancer treatments could also be used. As little as a measuring cup's worth of radioactive material would be needed, though small amounts probably would not cause severe harm, especially if scattered over a wide area.

In the event of a dirty bomb attack, some likely roles for CCMRF may be:

1. Radiation assessment. Others may also be involved, including the Defense Threat Reduction Agency (DTRA), Air Force Radiation Assessment Team (AFRAT), National Guard WMD-Civil Support Teams (WMD-CSTs), CERFP units, assigned Chemical companies and Federal civilian agencies such as the National Atmospheric Release Advisory Center (NARAC), Radiological Assistance Program (RAP), Aerial Measuring System (AMS).

2. Determining the borders of the contaminated area.

3. Decontamination. This may include not only people, but other objects in the contaminated area such as buildings, vehicles, etc.

4. Medical care. In a radiological attack, the number of actual injuries and radiological contaminations may be less than the number of "worried well." Still, planning should take these "worried well" into account, in the interest of maintaining public trust and confidence.

PHASE II: STAGING

In the event of a significant CBRNE incident, "lean forward" in anticipation of a potential deployment:

- Check equipment

- Maintain communications with your chain of command

- Review civilian and military incident command structures

- Monitor News Reports: Give particular attention to nature of public response (remember the Strategic Center of Gravity).

- Research type of CBRNE threat reported.

- Research incident location.

- Based on research, exercises, past experiences, and other outcomes of the Shaping Stage work to envision multiple response scenarios and options. Prepare your mind for a range of possibilities.

Phase 2: **STAGING**

Clarify the nature and impact of the event.

Actions
- NSAT deployment
- coordination with state and local officials
- JPAC employment ISO other HQs
- response forces positioned and/or postured to facilitate quick response

Main Effort
- NORTHCOM Situational Awareness Team (NSAT)

Phase 2 begins with
- identification of a potential CBRNE-CM incident or when directed by Commander USARNORTH

Phase II: STAGING

For many CCMRF units, transition from Shaping to Staging will take place when news media begin reporting a possible CBRNE event and when the nature and impact of the event are not yet clear.

Clarifying the nature and impact of the event is the purpose of Stage II. Whenever a possible CBRNE event occurs within the United States the JTF-CS intelligence unit stands up an Incident Analysis Cell (IAC). Using a pre-developed CM Area Assessment for the site of the CBRNE event, if available, the IAC seeks to develop hazard area modeling and works to depict the event over time.

JTF-CS OPLAN 0500 explains, "Phase II begins with the identification of a potential CBRNE incident or when directed by Commander USARNORTH thru the issuance of an EXORD/DEPORD. This phase ends when CCMRF receives prepare-to-deploy order or when NSAT determines scope and magnitude does not warrant CCMRF employment. Phase II success equals NSAT deployment, coordination with state and local officials, JPAC employment ISO other HQs, and response forces positioned and/or postured to facilitate quick response. Main effort during this phase is NORTHCOM Situational Awareness Team (NSAT)."

The **NORTHCOM Situational Awareness Team (NSAT)** is usually deployed in coordination with FEMA or whatever primary agency is designated by the President.

Following coordination with state civil and military officials and Federal officials, the NSAT makes an evaluation of potential short-falls in Federal and state capabilities, which may become requests for DOD assistance."

"The NSAT prepares its assessment shaped by its knowledge of CBRNE effects, the harm or damage they may cause, and how to mitigate and manage the resulting consequences. The assessment identifies proposed methods of response, anticipated actions, and potentially required forces." (JP 3-41, page IV-2)

NSAT is designed to give the Combatant Commander a standing capability to receive operational and tactical level awareness and assessment.

Specific NSAT assessment items include:

- Damage and injury reports
- Nature of the incident
- Force protection
- Duration and geographical extent of the incident
- Weather and terrain
- Public reaction
- Mission duration
- CBRNE Reconnaissance measures
- Identification of supporting DOD forces

As part of staging, Liaison Officers are alerted and deployed to the State Emergency Operations Center, State National Guard Headquarters, the Regional Response Command Center, and Joint Field Office, as applicable, to contribute to the Commander's Assessment. Emergency Preparedness Liaison Officers (EPLOs) are Reservists (Army, Air Force and Navy) that drill each month. They serve as eyes and ears for the Defense Coordinating Officer (DCO) and Defense Coordinating Element (DCE). Regional Emergency Preparedness Liaison Officers (REPLOs) are assigned and drill at the FEMA Regional Office; and State Emergency Preparedness Officers (SEPLOs) drill each month at each State National Guard Headquarters. "EPLOs" is the term given to all of them for training and conferences.

While the NSAT is doing its work, CCMRF units prepare to deploy (JTF-CS OPLAN 0500, page D-5). For example, during Phase II medical units "actively coordinate with regional and state authorities, preparing for potential transition" to Stage III and beyond. Crisis action planning begins for Health Service Support (HSS), "including HSS Measures of Performance and Measures of Effectiveness." (JTF-CS OPLAN 0500, page Q-9). Other units will apply situational awareness to begin the process of developing similar measurable objectives appropriate for their capabilities and role.

All CCMRF units "adjust CBRNE Response Posture Level (CRPL) as directed by CDRUSNORTHCOM and complete remaining training and preparation. Force providers provide assessments of unit mission readiness through DRRS to USARNORTH. Prepare to deploy." (JTF-CS OPLAN 0500, page 26)

For most CCMRF units the Staging Phase does not alter standing orders or current assignments. But as part of proactive Shaping — and to be fully poised for Phase III — unit commanders should actively monitor unfolding events, ensure full readiness, and focus situational awareness on the nature of the catastrophic event being reported by the news media and in information provided through the chain of command. In some cases, CCMRF units may be asked to "lean forward" and make preparations for deployment even if no EXORD has yet been issued. The Defense Coordinating Officer, ARNORTH and NORTHCOM will be involved in this decision.

DIRTY BOMB

Staging
for a Dirty Bomb Attack

• What is the NSAT likely to encounter following a dirty bomb explosion?

From the television program NOVA:

NOVA: What kind of response would there be if a dirty bomb attack occurred...?

Dr. Allison: "If the blast is very small, let's say a stick of dynamite, and the material is not highly radioactive, the impact would be relatively small. Say you and I were in this room, and one stick of dynamite went off under my chair. I probably would be blown up, and you probably would be harmed, and you would get some amount of rads. But you get a certain amount of rads every-day from walking around in the sun or from getting a medical procedure. So I think the question would depend on the strength and intensity of the various items. The first-ever dirty bomb attack would be a dramatic event, I suspect, because people wouldn't know quite what to make of it. Lots of people are confused about what is a dirty bomb and what is a nuclear weapon. They might mistakenly think that a nuclear weapon had gone off."

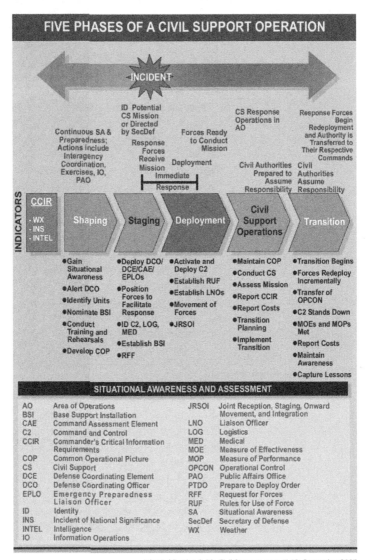

FIVE PHASES OF A CIVIL SUPPORT OPERATION

INCIDENT

Continuous SA & Preparedness; Actions include Interagency Coordination, Exercises, IO, PAO

ID Potential CS Mission or Directed by SecDef Response Forces Receive Mission Immediate Response

Forces Ready to Conduct Mission Deployment

CS Response Operations in AO Civil Authorities Prepared to Assume Responsibility

Response Forces Begin Redeployment and Authority is Transferred to Their Respective Commands Civil Authorities Assume Responsibility

INDICATORS

CCIR
- WX
- INS
- INTEL

Shaping | Staging | Deployment | Civil Support Operations | Transition

- ●Gain Situational Awareness
- ●Alert DCO
- ●Identify Units
- ●Nominate BSI
- ●Conduct Training and Rehearsals
- ●Develop COP

- ●Deploy DCO/ DCE/CAE/ EPLOs
- ●Position Forces to Facilitate Response
- ●ID C2, LOG, MED
- ●Establish BSI
- ●RFF

- ●Activate and Deploy C2
- ●Establish RUF
- ●Establish LNOs
- ●Movement of Forces
- ●JRSOI

- ●Maintain COP
- ●Conduct CS
- ●Assess Mission
- ●Report CCIR
- ●Report Costs
- ●Transition Planning
- ●Implement Transition

- ●Transition Begins
- ●Forces Redeploy Incrementally
- ●Transfer of OPCON
- ●C2 Stands Down
- ●MOEs and MOPs Met
- ●Report Costs
- ●Maintain Awareness
- ●Capture Lessons

SITUATIONAL AWARENESS AND ASSESSMENT

AO	Area of Operations	JRSOI	Joint Reception, Staging, Onward Movement, and Integration
BSI	Base Support Installation		
CAE	Command Assessment Element	LNO	Liaison Officer
C2	Command and Control	LOG	Logistics
CCIR	Commander's Critical Information Requirements	MED	Medical
		MOE	Measure of Effectiveness
COP	Common Operational Picture	MOP	Measure of Performance
CS	Civil Support	OPCON	Operational Control
DCE	Defense Coordinating Element	PAO	Public Affairs Office
DCO	Defense Coordinating Officer	PTDO	Prepare to Deploy Order
EPLO	Emergency Preparedness Liaison Officer	RFF	Request for Forces
		RUF	Rules for Use of Force
ID	Identity	SA	Situational Awareness
INS	Incident of National Significance	SecDef	Secretary of Defense
INTEL	Intelligence	WX	Weather
IO	Information Operations		

Joint Publication 3-28. Civil Support, page III-12, September 2007

Phase III: DEPLOYMENT

If the NSAT finds sufficient need the Commander of the Joint Task Force-Civil Support will request assignment of CCMRF units. The USNORTHCOM Combatant Commander will issue an EXORD and a Prepare-to-Deploy order. The Joint Task Force-Civil Support will delineate the transfer of forces and the requirements associated with the delegation of command authority in the **Operations Order (OPORD)** or subsequent orders during Crisis Action Planning. "Time from deployment of the NSAT to submission of Commander's Assessment of potential CBRNE incident through completion of execution

PHASE III: DEPLOYMENT

• Be ready.

• Use time in transit and assembling to advance readiness:
  – Review Capabilities.
  – Review Orders.
  – Review Standing Rules for the Use of Force.
  – Review principles and strategies outlined in this book.
  – Think through measurable objectives.
  – Focus on how your unit's capabilities can best affect the Strategic Center of Gravity.

• See Annex for Planning Checklists.

planning and transition to Phase III (Deployment) may be 6 to 96 hours." (JTF-CS OPLAN 0500, page C-8) The duration of deployment depends on the size of the response required, availability of transportation, local support infrastructure, proximity of ports of debarkation to the CBRNE incident site.

"The purpose of Phase III is to execute deployment of forces to the Joint Operations Area in order to save lives, mitigate the effects of the CBNRE incident and provide temporary critical support to the local populace. Phase III begins with JTF-CS and CCMRF deployment, however, force deployment can occur through all phases of this OPLAN, except Phase I, Shaping. Because of the nature of CBRNE Consequence

Management operations, forces will likely deploy into and out of the JOA for the entire length of the CBRNE CM operation." (JTF-CS OPLAN 0500, page ix)

Much of Phase III is focused on transportation of military personnel and materiel to the disaster site. If possible, a **Base Support Installation (BSI)** will be designated. But if a BSI is not available CCMRF units must be prepared to utilize their own rations, tents and equipment until full logistic capabilities are available.

Once the multiple units begin arriving at the **Port of Debarkation (POD)** a crucial aspect of deployment is to integrate subordinate units into the overall force. Serious and sustained engagement in the Shaping Phase will support an effective integration process. Being aware of the standing OPLAN, training to the OPLAN, and exercising to OPLAN will facilitate the varied units deploying in a manner ready to achieve unity of command.

Joint Doctrine defines **integration** as **the synchronized transfer of mission-ready units into the combatant commander's force**. Integration may take hours or days. The complexity and time required for integration depends on the size, contingency conditions, and coordination and planning. C2, communications, and security are the priority of effort during the integration phase. **Integration is complete when the receiving commander establishes command and control over the arriving unit and the unit is capable of performing its assigned mission.** (JP 4-01.8, page VII-1)

The CCMRF is unlikely to be deployed unless the nation is facing a disaster with potentially catastrophic consequences. There will be an urgent need to complete deployments as quickly as possible.

Deploying to a Dirty Bomb Attack

Given the limited physical impact and comparatively modest radiological dispersion of a dirty bomb, the NSAT may advise against deployment of the CCMRF. Many large city hazardous materials squads are capable of responding, and local medical capacity may be sufficient. National Guard resources — especially the CBRNE Enhanced Response Force Package (CERFP) — will be utilized before the CCMRF.

But it is also possible that some specialized CCMRF units will be deployed. The presence of CCMRF units may be helpful in reassuring the public and demonstrating the responsiveness of authorities to the event.

- If local authorities are substantively capable of response, what is the role of the CCMRF?

- What is the Strategic Center of Gravity?

- How can CCMRF units and personnel contribute to engaging the Strategic Center of Gravity?

- In this more modest response, what is the likely chain-of-command?

DIRTY BOMB

Soldiers check an AH-64 Apache Longbow at Fort Bliss, Texas, before conducting an aerial reconnaissance flight. Source: northcom.mil, photo by Edd Natividad.

111

Phase IV:
CIVIL SUPPORT OPERATIONS

As CCMRF units confirm mission readiness they will begin Civil Support Operations. Depending on the nature of the disaster, the situation on the ground, specific Mission Assignments (MA's), and CCMRF capabilities, taskings will be sequenced as units arrive in the JOA.

"The purpose of Phase IV is to conduct CBRNE-CM operations in support of Civil Authorities in the execution of approved Mission Assignments (MAs) in order to save lives, prevent injury, and provide temporary life support." (JTF-CS OPLAN 0500, C-12)

The range of taskings will include:

• Logistics and distribution
• Citizen evacuation
• Support of displaced population
• Mortuary operations
• Clearing major transportation routes
• Hazard surveying and monitoring
• Decontamination
• Search and Rescue (extraction)
• Medical transport
• Medical services
• Public affairs

There will be many more taskings as a Common Operating Picture is established and priority needs are identified. As operations proceed every unit can contribute to expanding the Common Operating Picture and ensuring its accuracy. The OPLAN anticipates that it will not be possible to achieve a detailed and credible Common Operating Picture for 24 to 48 hours (or longer) after the incident. The more quickly a COP can be achieved the more effectively consequence management operations can be employed.

Give special effort to sharing information up the chain of command related to the **Commander's Critical Information Requirements (CCIR) such as these examples**:

• Are there credible indications and warnings of impending or actual incident(s) involving terrorism or CBRNE?

• Are there any situational changes that should affect ongoing Phase II and III operations?

• Are there any shortfalls in CCMRF critical equipment/personnel capabilities?

• Are there any force protection risks in the Joint Operating Area?

• Are any CCMRF units reaching the established limit for operational exposure? (See Annex for details)

Providing this information up the chain-of-command as quickly as possible is especially important given the very high risks involved in Catastrophic Consequence Management. Plans assume that "movement of forces from staging areas into mission areas may be affected by infrastructure failures, self-evacuating populace, panic, civil disturbances, and contaminated environments. **Mitigation of risk during CBRNE CM operations involves in-depth knowledge of the operating environment and timely situational awareness.**" (JTF-CS OPLAN 0500, page 28) This depends on constant communications between all tactical units and headquarters.

Coordination with civilian authorities is also critically important. But **the military chain-of-command does not change**. Your orders come through military channels, not through civilian incident command. Military liaison with civilian authority is critically important, but liaison is not C2. The Principal Federal Agency and Principal Federal Officer will almost always be civilian. But this does not change the authority of the combatant commander or JTF commander. All Mission Assignments (MAs) for the military will come from the Federal

Coordinating Officer (FCO), through the Defense Coordinating Officer (DCO). The DCO is the single point of contact for the military on the ground. The DCO will forward the MA to the JTF, who will then task Title 10 unit/s to complete the MA.

M.A.C.H.I.N.E.

The unpredictable operational environment of consequence management can be successfully engaged if CCMRF personnel consistently apply seven key lessons-learned. Success comes from:

Mission Focus
Attention to Capabilities
Communicating
Harmonizing
Insisting on Professionalism
Never being Surprised
Establishing a Ready Reserve

Your orders will communicate the mission and end-state. This book has communicated the doctrine, strategy, and principles that are to be applied. Your commander will communicate a vision and intention. **You should know your mission.** But once you roll on scene to execute the mission your organization will become the go-to folks. **Beware of mission creep.** Be clear with yourself, with your unit, and with those who you are working to serve regarding the core components of your mission and why, for the greater good, it is very important to keep your focus on achieving that mission. Remember: Mission Assignments (MAs) and/or taskings will come from the JTF for Title 10 units.

The subordinate units of the CCMRF have been brought together for a specific mission. **The capabilities assembled are designed to achieve a particular end-state.** You have been given orders to apply these specific capabilities in a way that contributes to an overall Consequence Management effort. Applying your capabilities to a different purpose can distract from and delay achievement of mission.

114

M.A.C.H.I.N.E.

- **M**ission Focus
- **A**ttention to Capabilities
- **C**ommunicating
- **H**armonizing
- **I**nsisting on Professionalism
- **N**ever being Surprised
- **E**stablishing a Ready Reserve

Public Trust

In some circumstances **you can endanger your capabilities and per-sonnel by taking on tasks for which you have not been trained**. By being attentive — and realistic — regarding your capabilities you are most likely to contribute to mission success.

Informing local citizens and response personnel of your mission and capabilities, staying in close contact with other responders — civilian and military — and reporting up the chain-of-command on progress or challenges are all crucial to mission success. **You are engaged in 360 degree communications:** vertical, horizontal, and in three dimensions. In most cases requests for action that do not match your specific capa-bilities can be positively answered by communicating through the chain-of-command and in coordination with civilian incident command to have forces with task-appropriate capabilities assigned to the request. With effective communications you can be responsive and effective without necessarily doing the job yourself.

The purpose of this ongoing communication is to achieve unity of command and unity of effort. You are helping to harmonize a thousand moving pieces in an overall response to a catastrophe. The goal is for your capabilities to complement other capabilities already responding or preparing to respond. The goal is for military and civilian response efforts to be effectively coordinated on priority tasks.

Remember the Strategic Center of Gravity: public trust. The profes-sionalism of military personnel — how they look, behave, and communi-cate — is a significant element in achieving the SCG. A key element in the professionalism of a US military officer is his or her deference to the Constitution. Especially in Civil Support Operations the military is not in charge. The military has been assigned to support civil authorities. Clarity and consistency in this professional role is fundamental to mission success.

Expect the unexpected. Be prepared for anything. Recognize you are moving into a high-risk environment that will present unpredictable demands. The key is **being creative and principled in responding to the tough problems that unfold**. This is why doctrine gives so much attention to strategy, principles, and measurable objectives. Procedures do not exist to solve many of the problems that will emerge. You are expected to develop principled solutions.

One of the best ways to expect the unexpected is to **maintain a ready reserve**. This is an important choice at both the battalion and brigade level. This may involve not tasking some units, which given the intense challenges of consequence management may seem counter-intuitive. But **the unexpected will happen**. Unless sufficient forces can be rapidly applied to the unexpected the problem may escalate out of control. As Churchill said, "those who wait also serve."

The seven lessons of MACHINE have been proven again and again in Civil Support Operations over the years. That does not mean they are easy lessons to learn or to consistently apply.

Public Affairs

The media will play an important role shaping the Strategic Center for Gravity. "Any DOD response must take into account possible media contributions and repercussions." (JTF-CS OPLAN 0500, page 39) The JFO Joint Information Center will be the principal point of contact for the media.

The Public Affairs unit attached to JTF-CS will assume an active posture. But it is likely that the media will approach individual military units and personnel. The Army Field Manual for Civil Support **Operations offers the following media guidelines:**

Commanders or senior staff members grant interviews. These interviews serve as opportunities to ensure the public receives accurate, timely, and useful information.

CCMRF members maintain a professional attitude. CCMRF members remain in control even when a news media representative seems aggressive or asks seemingly silly questions. CCMRF members are polite but firm and use simple, concise language free of military jargon and acronyms.

CCMRF members make a good impression. CCMRF members speaking to the news media relax and behave naturally. They ignore cameras and talk directly to the reporter. They remove sunglasses and headgear if appropriate. They use appropriate posture and gestures.

CCMRF members think before speaking. CCMRF members always pause and think before answering. They answer questions accurately, but not necessarily instantly. They answer one question at a time. They do not allow anyone to badger, harass, or pressure them into answering. They do not get angry. CCMRF members do not answer "what if" (speculative) questions or offer personal opinions.

CCMRF members understand the question. If a question seems unclear, a CCMRF member asks the reporter to rephrase it. CCMRF members give consistent and accurate answers.

Everything is on the record. Every word spoken to a news media representative is on the record. CCMRF members may be friendly but businesslike. They only discuss the current civil support operation. The interviewer chooses the questions; the CCMRF member chooses the answers.

Questions do not appear in the final news product. Videotape, radio, internet, and print media are known to edit their questions so the audience only hears or reads the CCMRF member's answer. The answer may stand alone. However, if an interviewer uses a loaded catch phrase, such as "assassination squad," the CCMRF member does not use the same expression in the answer. Sample question: "What are you doing about the assassination squads?" Sample answer: "We are committed to investigating this matter and may take the necessary and appropriate action."

CCMRF members speak about what they know. If the information sought by a reporter is not known, the CCMRF member's reply is, "I don't know." That answer rarely appears in print. CCMRF members avoid speculation. They avoid answering a question that may be more appropriate for another individual. CCMRF members talk about their area of expertise. When possible, CCMRF members direct a reporter to the most appropriate

individual with the required knowledge.
CCMRF members tell the truth.
A CCMRF member does not try to cover embarrassing events with a security classification. It is never appropriate to lie to the media. (Draft FM 3-28, page G-3)

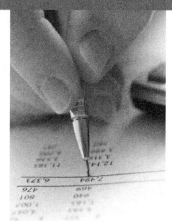

Financial Reimbursement

According to Joint Doctrine,
"All DOD Support is provided on a reimbursable basis, unless otherwise directed by the President or reimbursement is waived by the Secretary of Defense. In most cases, state, local, and federal agencies provide reimbursement for assistance provided by DOD. The reimbursement process requires the DOD components to capture and report total and incremental costs in accordance with applicable DOD financial regulations." (JP 3-28, page A-2)

The principal DOD financial regulation for Civil Support Operations is DOD 7000.14-R. Generally, **CCMRF units can expect to collect the following financial and background information:**

• Record of missions performed.
• Rosters of personnel involved.
• Travel and per diem (military and civil service).
• Civilian employee overtime
• Temporary personnel wages, travel, and per diem.
• Lodging cost.
• Transportation cost (car and bus rentals, chartered aircraft, fuel).
• Contracting cost.
• Equipment provided or operated (estimated hourly cost for operation).
• Material provided from regular stock. (all classes of supply).
• Laundry expenses.
• Official or morale phone calls.

- Retain receipts and other supporting documents. Supporting documents include:
  - Unit orders
  - Temporary duty (TDY) orders
  - TDY payment vouchers
  - Vehicle dispatch logs
  - Fuel card receipts
  - Hand receipts
  - Request and receipt of supplies
  - Government credit card receipts
  - Copy of contracts
  - Memorandums and other documentation of exceptions to policy/regulations
  - Mortuary services. (Draft FM 3-28, page B-4)

Joint Doctrine has also identified several activities that are usually **non-reimbursable**. These include:

- Regular pay and allowances of military and civilian personnel
- Charges for use of military vehicles and watercraft
- Aircraft, vehicles, or watercraft damaged, lost, destroyed, or abandoned
- Administrative overhead
- Annual and sick leave, retirement, and other benefits
- Cost of communications used to requisition items in a disaster area to replenish stocks. (JP 3-28, page A-2)

Complete and accurate accounting of these expenses and activities is another element in preserving public trust.

JTF-CS OPLAN 0500 includes detailed planning assumptions and suggestions for a wide range of operations. There are separate annexes for most key functions. In the annex to this book please see planning checklists.

Phase IV ends with CBRNE effects reduced and conditions set for transition of operations to civil authorities or designated command. "Success equals civil authorities ready to respond effectively to continuing requirements." (JTF-CS OPLAN 0500, page 28)

DIRTY BOMB

Operations
for a Dirty Bomb Attack

From the television program NOVA:

Dr Graham Allison is director of the Belfer Center for Science and International Affairs at Harvard University and former Assistant Secretary of Defense under President Clinton.

NOVA: So if a fairly sizable dirty bomb went off in the center of Boston on a windy day, and a lot of people were exposed to its radiation, would people be at all equipped to deal with it?

Dr. Allison: I suspect not, because they probably haven't been well-informed. They would quickly go to a Web site to try to see what they could learn about it…But there would be general confusion, as unfortunately there would be for most terrorist acts at this stage, given on the one hand the absence of an effective education process for people, and on the other the desire not to know too much about this.

Given Dr. Alison's description, what is the most important role of CCMRF units and personnel in responding to a dirty bomb explosion?

Using the MACHINE set of lessons-learned, communicating and insisting on professionalism will be especially valuable. By demonstrating and discussing the limited impact of a dirty bomb CCMRF personnel can reduce public confusion, uncertainty, and fear.

Phase V: TRANSITION

JTF-CS OPLAN 0500 explains, the purpose of Phase V "is for DOD forces to redeploy to home station, reset, and reconstitute.... This phase will occur concurrently with Phase IV. The phase ends when CJT-FCS transfers C2 of DOD CM operations to the Defense Coordinating Officer or designated DOD C2 Headquarters. Success equals a complete transfer of responsibilities to civil authorities." (JTF-CS OPLAN 0500, page 29)

This is what Phase V is about. This is the goal that you should discuss with your civilian colleagues from Phase I forward and during every element of Phase IV. "Success equals a complete transfer of responsibilities to civil authorities."

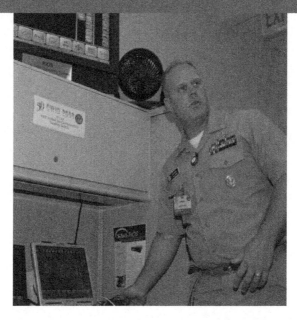

ABOVE:
Chief Information Systems Technician Michael Layman demonstrated the Radio Interoperability System, a computer based technology which allows military and civil-band radios as well as cell-phones and even internet-based communications systems to interlink and communicate one with another during the Coalition Warrior Interoperability Demonstration 2008 at U.S. Northern Command. Source: northcom.mil, photo by Petty Officer 1st Class Joaquin Juatai.

LEFT:
MINNEAPOLIS, Minn. — Secretary of Transportation, Mary E. Peters, tours the site of the I-35 bridge collapse over the Mississippi river with Col. Michael Chesney, defense coordinating officer (DCO), August 10, 2007. The DCO is responsible for coordination of Department of Defense personnel and equipment in support of civil authorities in the case of a disaster response operation. Source: northcom.mil, photo by Seaman Joshua Adam Nuzzo.

ANNEX

ANNEX

- **Standing Rules of the Use of Force**
  Source: Appendix B of Joint Publication (JP) 3-28 Civil Support

- **Planning Checklists**
  Source: Appendix B of Army Field Manual (Draft FM) 3-28 Civil Support Operations

- **Operational Risk Management Guidelines**
  Source: US Army Health CBRN Guidelines

- **The Stafford Act**
  Source: Joint Publication 3-28

- **Posse Comitatus Act**
  Source: Joint Publication 3-41

- **Logistics and CCMRF**
  Source: ARNORTH White Paper

- **Glossary**
  Source: JTF-CS OPLAN 0500

- **Interim Evaluation**

CBRNE Chemical, Biological, Radiological, Nuclear and high-yield Explosive threats

▪ Standing Rules for the Use of Force

(Source: Appendix B of Joint Publication (JP) 3-28 Civil Support)

Note: All CCMRF members should identify legal restraints and constraints affecting any CCMRF mission.

1. Purpose

Although projecting power overseas has been the usual strategy for ensuring national security, the evolution of new threats against the nation has caused DOD to reshape its approach to this important task. In this era of potential domestic terrorism and natural disasters, US military forces may be required to assist civil authorities and to use force in the very heart of the nation. The participation of the military in such scenarios is fraught with legal and political pitfalls that warrant clear and specific guidance on the use of force. Third parties may seek to exacerbate a situation for their own purposes by provoking an excessive use of force. The purpose of this Appendix is to publish fundamental policies and procedures governing the RUF by DOD forces during domestic CS missions. These RUF do not apply to NG forces while in state active duty or Title 32 USC status.

2. Policy

a. CJCSI 3121.01B, *Standing Rules of Engagement/Standing Rules for the Use of Force for US Forces*, establishes fundamental policies and procedures governing the actions to be taken by US commanders and their forces during all DOD CS and routine military department functions occurring within the US territory or US territorial seas. SRUF also apply to land HD missions occurring within US territory.

b. The SecDef approves and the CJCS promulgates standing rules of engagement (SROE) and SRUF for US forces. The Joint Staff, Operations Directorate is responsible for the maintenance of the SROE/SRUF in coordination with OSD. Commanders at all levels are responsible for establishing rules of engagement (ROE)/RUF for mission accomplishment that comply with the ROE/RUF of senior commanders, the law of armed conflict, applicable international and domestic law and the CJCS SROE/ SRUF. It is critical that commanders consult with their command judge advocates when establishing ROE/RUF.

c. Unless otherwise directed by a unit commander (IAW CJCSI 3121.01B, *Standing Rules of Engagement/Standing Rules for the Use of Force for US Forces*), military personnel have the right under law to use force that is reasonably necessary under the circumstances to defend themselves against violent, dangerous or life-threatening personal attack. In addition, military personnel are authorized to use force to discharge certain duties.

d. Nothing in this Appendix alters or limits military commanders' inherent right and obligation to exercise unit self-defense in response to a hostile act or demonstrated hostile intent. Unit self-defense includes the defense of other DOD forces in the vicinity.

e. Commanders at all levels are responsible for training their personnel to understand and properly utilize the SRUF. In this regard, it is critical that legal advisers be available to assist in this training and to advise commanders at all levels of the applicable rules.

f. When DOD forces are detailed to other federal agencies, mission-specific RUF will be used. These RUF must be approved by the SecDef and the federal agency concerned.

g. DOD units under USCG control and conducting law enforcement support operations or maritime homeland security support operations will follow the Coast Guard Use of Force Policy, Commandant, United States Coast Guard Instruction 16247.1, *US Coast Guard Maritime Law Enforcement Manual* for employing warning shots and disabling fire, and follow the SROE/SRUF and/or mission specific use of force rules for all other purpose. However, DOD forces under USCG control retain the right of self-defense.

h. When DOD forces under DOD control operate in coordination with other federal agencies, the applicable RUF will be coordinated with the on-scene federal agency personnel.

i. CCDRs may augment these SRUF as necessary by submitting

"It is an unbending rule of law, that the exercise of military power, where the rights of the citizen are concerned, shall never be pushed beyond what the exigency requires."

— Associate Justice of the Supreme Court Noah Swayne, Raymond v. Thomas, 91 US 712, 716 (1875)

requests for mission specific RUF to the CJCS, for approval by the SecDef (IAW CJCSI 3121.01B, Standing Rules of Engagement/ Standing Rules for the Use of Force for US Forces).

3. Procedures

Normally, force is to be used only as a last resort, and should be the minimum necessary. The use of force must be reasonable in intensity, duration, and magnitude based on the totality of the circumstances to counter the threat. If force is required, nonlethal force is authorized and may be used to control a situation and accomplish the mission, or to provide self-defense of DOD forces, defense of non-DOD persons in the vicinity if directly related to the assigned mission, or in defense of the protected property, when doing so is reasonable under the circumstances. Lethal force is authorized only when all lesser means have failed or cannot reason-ably be employed and the circumstances otherwise justify the use of lethal force.

a. General direction regarding the appropriate use of force comes from a conceptual framework known as the "Use of Force Continuum." The Use of Force Continuum is generally seamless and does not require movement from one level to the next in sequential order. The Use of Force Continuum can be divided into five broad categories related to the goals of the military units providing support

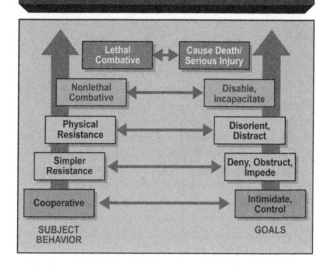

CONTINUUM OF FORCE LEVELS

and behavior of subject audience. They are: Intimidate/Control, Deny/Obstruct/Impede, Disorient/Distract, Disable/Incapacitate, and Cause Death/Serious Injury **(see Chart on right)**.

(1) **Intimidate/Control.** In most cases, the subject audience will comply with the verbal instructions or commands. When time and circumstances permit, the individual(s) or group should be warned and given the opportunity to withdraw with the goal of preventing the escalation of force. Verbal commands used with firmness and tact should be sufficient to control the situation. Additionally, the military unit's resolve can be implied by mere presence, donning protective gear, or forming into riot control formations.

(2) **Deny/Obstruct/Impede.** At this level, the subject audience exhibits usually simple resistance or refusal to obey instructions and there is no immediate danger of a physical confrontation. The use of tactics, techniques and procedures to deny the subject audience presence in or access to an area or to obstruct or impede their movement is authorized. Examples of the methods

short of physical contact include the use of concertina, caltrops, or other means to barricade or isolate an area.

(3) Disorient/Distract. At this level, actual physical resistance may be encountered. Resistance is commonly manifested by continued refusal to comply with directions coupled with threatening behavior, shouting and open defiance. The use of nonlethal weapons (NLWs) that cause physical disorientation and distraction may be authorized by the appropriate approval authority.

(4) Disable/Incapacitate. This is the level at which military personnel are in imminent danger of bodily injury. It is generally characterized by the subject audience using physical attacks or other combative actions to prevent apprehension or otherwise frustrate military operations. The use of Service-approved, unit-issued NLWs that cause physical discomfort, physical incapacitation or blunt trauma are authorized. Detailed guidance for use of riot control agents by DOD personnel is governed by CJCSI 3110.07C, *Guidance Concerning the Chemical, Biological, Radiological, and Nuclear Defense and Employment of Riot Control Agents and Herbicides* (S). Although the use of NLWs that cause physical discomfort may fall short of inflicting actual trauma, the employment of these weapons requires nevertheless an assessment of reasonableness under the circumstances. NLWs that inflict blunt trauma constitute the most serious of the nonlethal options within the Use of Force Continuum. Care should be exercised in employing such options as they may cause painful or debilitating injuries, and in some rare cases, death.

(5) Cause Death/Serious Injury. In the final level of the Use of Force Continuum, the subject audience behaves in a manner that is combative and poses an imminent threat of death or serious bodily harm. In such cases, DOD forces may respond with lethal force. While lethal force is to be used only when all lesser means have failed or cannot reasonably be employed, lethal force is authorized under the following circumstances:

(a) Lethal force is authorized when DOD unit commanders reasonably believe there is an imminent threat of death or serious bodily harm to their units and other DOD forces in the vicinity.

(b) Lethal force is authorized in defense of non-DOD persons in the vicinity, when directly related to the assigned mission.

(c) Lethal force is authorized when lethal force reasonably appears to be necessary to prevent the actual theft or sabotage of **assets vital to national security**.

(d) Lethal force is authorized when lethal force reasonably appears to be necessary to prevent the actual theft or sabotage of inherently dangerous property.

(e) Lethal force is authorized when lethal force reasonably appears to be necessary to prevent the sabotage of national critical infrastructure.

b. Consequently, when directly related to the assigned mission, lethal force is authorized under the following circumstances:

(1) Lethal force is authorized when lethal force reasonably appears to be necessary to prevent the commission of a serious offense that involves imminent threat of death or serious bodily harm (for example, setting fire to an inhabited dwelling or sniping), including the defense of other persons, where lethal force is directed against the person threatening to commit the offense. Examples include murder, armed robbery and aggravated assault.

(2) Lethal force is authorized when lethal force reasonably appears to be necessary to prevent the escape of a prisoner, provided there is probable cause to believe that such person(s) have committed or attempted to commit a serious offense, that is, one that involves imminent threat of death or serious bodily harm, and would pose an imminent threat of death or serious bodily harm to DOD forces or others in the vicinity.

(3) Lethal force is authorized when lethal force reasonably appears necessary to arrest or apprehend a person who, there is probable cause to believe, has committed a serious offense (as defined in the preceding subparagraph).

c. When operating under these RUF, warning shots are not authorized within US territory (including US territorial waters), except when in the appropriate exercise of force protection of US Navy and Naval Service vessels during maritime operations as permitted by CJCSI 3121.01B, *Standing Rules of Engagement/Standing Rules for the Use of Force for US Forces*.

d. Units with assigned weapons may deploy with weapons stored; however, weapons will not be carried during CS operations unless authorized by the SecDef.

▪ Planning Checklists

(Source: Appendix B of Army Field Manual (Draft FM) 3-28 Civil Support Operations)

STAFF CHECKLISTS

Planning Checklist for S1, Human Resources

S1 performs checks on the following —

• Deployment orders

• Personnel accountability, including an accountability system encompassing surge capacity for additional government, contractor, and volunteer personnel

• Medical requirements

• Preparation for movement: medical records, including dental and shot records, insurance documents, powers of attorney, wills, etc.

• Postal service

• Pay/finance, to include civilian pay adjustments

• Mortuary affairs

• Chaplain access, notification procedures established for loss of life and injury

• Automation equipment including power generation, back-up battery packs with surge protection, photo copiers, printing capability with backup printer, field filing systems, supplies, tool kit, mobile shelving, tables, chairs, waterproof shelter, heating, cooling

Planning Checklist for S2, Intelligence

JTF-CS Directorate of Intelligence will perform the following tasks. CCMRF S2 should BPT contribute updates and integrate this information with their respective operational units.

- Intelligence preparation of the disaster area (modified intelligence preparation of the battlefield).

- Maps (paper and electronic) both civilian and military, electronic topographic capability. Knowledge to incorporate systems to build map products useable to help locate personnel and critical facilities or infrastructure in areas where road signs, roads, and landmarks are destroyed. Do military and Army civilian areas of responsibility (AORs) correlate? Is it possible to correlate AORs?

- Population demographics of residential areas. Residents of economically distressed areas are more likely to remain in the area and require support.

- Ethnic distribution of population in disaster areas; identify types of linguists required.

- Areas without electricity.

- Areas without water, status of water purification systems, and availability of commercial purification equipment and products, improvised water purification systems.

- Location and capabilities of medical facilities.

- Status of sanitation systems.

- Relief and drainage systems. Effects on mobility for unit vehicles in rescue and relief efforts. Estimated time to drain flooded areas; include bridging requirements if applicable.

- Obstacles. Identify areas where debris impedes mobility.

- Surface materials. Type and distribution of soils and subsoils in area and soil trafficability.

- Manmade features. Identify roads, railroads, bridges, tunnels, mines, towns, industrial areas, and piers. Identify unsafe structures requiring demolition.

S2 performs checks on the following:

- Availability of unmanned aircraft systems (UAS).

- Topographic systems with global positioning system and software.

- Operations and physical security.

- Arms room.

- Automation equipment including power generation, back-up battery packs with surge protection, photo copiers, printing capability with backup printer, field filing systems, supplies, tool kit, mobile shelving, tables, chairs, waterproof shelter, heating, cooling.

Initial Planning Checklist for S3, Operations

S3 performs checks on the following —

- Simple, concise definition of command and support relationships (Army and other coordinating organizations).

- Priority: location of victims requiring rescue, evacuation, and medical treatment; status of local emergency medical capabilities; hazards or potential threats; and facilities (such as schools or warehouses) for temporary housing.

- Status of lines of communication, major roads, railroads, waterways, ports, and airports in the area. State the nature and extent of damage and projected repairs.

- Characteristics of physical damage in specific areas: housing, commercial, industrial, public utilities, and so on. Start damage assessment in high-density and low-income areas: mobile homes, high-rise apartment buildings, and business offices.

• Numbers and locations of dislocated persons. Economically distressed areas tend to have more victims. These areas may be near industrial areas containing hazardous materials. Identify hazards such as fires, chemical spills, or ruptured pipelines.

Operational Planning Checklist for S3, Operations

S3 performs checks on the following —

• Local sources of media reproduction, especially high-speed, large-format printing.

• Availability of civilian engineer equipment and personnel.

• Advance party. Include signal officer, engineer, and internal logistics planner.

• Daily schedule.

• Briefings and reports.

• Points of contact for subject matter experts.

• Packing lists.

• Transportation (tactical)/convoy operations.

• Mission-related training and mission rehearsal exercises.

• Weapons qualification.

• After action reviews.

• Risk management.

• Liaison officers.

- Air command and control.

- Checks with S6 on Dedicated satellite/cell phones and satellite/cable Internet capability.

- Automation equipment including power generation, back-up battery packs with surge protection, photocopiers, printing capability, field filing systems, supplies, tool kit, mobile shelving, tables, chairs, waterproof shelter, heating, cooling.

Demobilization Planning Checklist for S3, Operations

S3 performs checks on the following —

- **Set end state conditions as soon as possible and recognize when the unit's work is complete.** Coordinate these conditions with other organizations. The Army responds to disasters when conditions temporarily overwhelm State and local governments.

- **Avoid Staying Too Long:**

  - State and local governments may expect Army assistance much longer than actually needed.
  - The Army avoids allowing state and local governments to become dependent on Army assistance, thus impeding long-term recovery.
  - If local businesses and contractors can perform the missions and tasks assigned to the Army, the continued employment of the Army may be unnecessary or illegal. It may rouse resentment of local citizens who feel deprived of employment opportunities.
  - The primary role of the Army is to train, prepare for, and execute combat operations. Even a short absence from this focus on combat operations may degrade a unit's preparedness.

- **End state and exit strategy tactics, techniques, and procedures include the following checks:**

- Be attentive to measures of performance and the conditions the Army achieves to declare mission success and the end state.
- Make clear to state and local governments that the Army presence is limited and temporary.
- Agree with state and local governments on the acceptable end state, usually recognized as when state and local governments can re-establish normal operations.
- Use commercial vendors and contractors.

Planning Checklist for S4, Sustainment (one of two)

S4 performs checks on the following —

- Sources of all classes of supply needed for critical restoration activities.

- Life support: mobile weatherproof shelters with all required equipment, billeting, mess, rations, water, bath and laundry.

- Funding. Fund sites, distribution of funding with other organizations.

- Transportation (administration). See chapter 2 of "Coordinating Military Deployments on Roads and Highways: A Guide for State and Local Agencies," dated May 2005, published by the U.S. Department of Transportation, Federal Highway Department, accessed at ops.fhwa.dot.gov/opssecurity on 3 January 2006.

- Petroleum, oils, and lubricants.

- Fuel access and fuel requirements.

- Minimum of a 90-day supply of repair parts based upon weather and increased use of certain types of equipment in unique environments.

- Locations/sources to purchase parts, fuel, oils, lubricants.
- Maintenance and recovery.

- Reception, staging, onward movement, and integration.

- Ammunition storage.

- Automation accessories required for austere environment.

Funding Planning Checklist for S4, Sustainment (two of two)

S4 performs checks on the following —

- In order for the Army to receive reimbursement, the supporting unit documents the support provided in a memorandum to their higher headquarters with S-4, G-8 involvement. The defense coordinating officer receives and validates a mission assignment. The mission assignment number is listed on request for reimbursement. The mission is executed using the supporting unit's operational funds.

- Maintain an accurate record of the mission. Items to include:

  - Record of missions performed.
  - Rosters of personnel involved.
  - Travel and per diem (military and civil service).
  - Civilian employee overtime
  - Temporary personnel wages, travel, and per diem.
  - Lodging cost.
  - Transportation cost (car and bus rentals, chartered aircraft, fuel).
  - Contracting cost.
  - Equipment provided or operated (estimated hourly cost for operation).
  - Material provided from regular stock. (all classes of supply).
  - Laundry expenses.
  - Official or morale phone calls.

- Retain receipts and other supporting documents. Supporting documents include:

  - Unit orders.
  - Temporary duty (TDY) orders.
  - TDY payment vouchers.
  - Vehicle dispatch logs.
  - Fuel card receipts.
  - Hand receipts.
  - Request and receipt of supplies.
  - Government credit card receipts.
  - Copy of contracts.
  - Memorandums and other documentation of exceptions to policy/regulations.
  - Mortuary services

Planning Checklist for C2, Command and Control Systems

C2 performs checks on the following —

- Coordinate with military (Air National Guard, Army National Guard, Coast Guard, Air Force, Navy, Marine Corps), local, state, Federal agencies and organizations and NGOs and volunteers. The bottom line is command control systems coordinate with virtually any agency, organization or individual that can help support the mission to reduce loss of life, limb and property. Determine the most feasible solutions for effective communication.
- Initial communications capabilities are self-sufficient and interoperable with both first responders and local authorities.
- Plan for all means of communications and purchasing of additional communication devices: telephone (satellite, cellular or land line), radio (military maritime, and civilian, in all band widths), Non-Secure Internet Protocol Router Network, SECRET Internet Protocol Router

Network, video equipment, video teleconferencing, and satellite-based commercial Internet systems. The goal is to communicate effectively and reduce restrictions to effective communication.

- Do not send equipment without operators, essential repair parts, operating and repair manuals, tools, initial fuel and power generation required.
- Send qualified signal leaders to ensure operators and equipment are used effectively.
- Prepare to provide communications equipment (cell phones, radios, base sets, etc.) to first responders.
- Plan and coordinate for additional, extended logistical and maintenance support for equipment and personnel as well as unexpected requirements including generator support; maintenance of equipment; fuel requirements of vehicles, systems, and generators; and support for others' equipment (i.e. charging cell phones from your power source, charging satellite phones, identify internal and external electronic repair capabilities).
- Know the power requirements for your equipment. Always bring your own power generation equipment, parts and fuel for essential communication equipment.
- Communications (voice, data, video) with various emergency operations centers including military (Air National Guard, Army National Guard, Coast Guard, Air Force, Navy, Marines), local, state, or federal.
- Communications structures are expandable and flexible to meet future needs. What can be established initially and expanded to handle a greater demand? Small deployable packages ahead of larger deployable command posts for immediate feedback of requirements.
- Establish reach-back capability.
- Conduct a synchronization meeting between all primary agencies/entities that have impact as soon as possible.
- Realize that geography and weather affects signal performance. A communications system that worked well at one location might not work in another.

STAFF JUDGE ADVOCATE CHECKLIST

Planning Checklist for SJA, Staff Judge Advocate

SJA performs checks on the following —

- Rules for the use of force.
  Review funding, demobilization, dangers, and entrance and exit strategies.

▪ Operational Risk Management Guidelines

Operational Risk Management Guideline:

Commanders need to do risk management. To do so effectively they should understand how the asymmetry of the impact of CBRN agents and their disproportionate effects on military assets (personnel, equipment, facilities, areas) make operational risk management following a CBRN event complex.

Factors Contributing to Operational Risk:

- The factors that make CBRN a risk to operational capability are more diverse than for other battlefield threats (the nature of CBRN agents, the multiple and effective ways of delivering them, the vastly differing times between exposure to the agent and the onset of symptoms, the difficulty in identifying the hazard area for some of the agents, the varying lengths of time that CBRN agents remain a hazard on various surfaces).
- CBRN events require disproportionate amounts of time and specialized resources to manage them and to survive and operate through events, generating losses in operational capability and operational timeline due to losses in personnel required to manage the event.

4S Category:

Sense

Operational Risk Management Guideline:

Commanders must take decisive action. Commanders will have to make operational decisions based on little or ambiguous information. It is critical to act quickly and decisively based on the information he have and the level of risk to operations that he is willing to accept, and to be ready to adjust his decision making as he gets more and better information on the event.

Factors Contributing to Operational Risk:

- Difficulty in determining that a CBRN event or attack has occurred and comprehensiveness of event/attack may degrade operations. You need to make a decision whether and how long you will operate in a knowledge vacuum before an event occurs.
- Post-event assessment of CBRN events requires anywhere from minutes (nuclear and chemical), to days or weeks (radiological and biological). This vastly increases the complexity of the decisions and the risk associated with them.

- Waiting until you have all the information to make a decision may seem wise, but it is usually better to act given what you know about the event and then to adjust your actions quickly and decisively as more knowledge becomes available.
- Planning and preparation underwrite your ability to do this.
- It is generally critical to know the following information:
  - Your decision making timeline given how quickly the agent will impact my assets and what I know about the time the event occurred
  - How long do you have to make decisions about operating?
  - How will agent characteristics (persistency, contagiousness, transmissibility, etc.) impact my OPSTEMPO and general operational capability?
  - Trigger event
  - Agent(s) involved in event
  - Delivery mechanism
  - When the event occurred (if possible)
  - Whether the event was deliberate, naturally occurring or an accident.
  - Mixture of personnel and assets (military, civilian, contractor – US and host nation, combined forces, allies, US citizens awaiting NEO, dependents, etc.) exposed to the event
  - Resources available to manage the event (i.e., physical protection, vaccinations, prophylaxis, medical treatment, etc.)
- Understanding what information is critical to making operational decision will help you to understand how high a risk your decision carries.
- You may even get information too late to take actions that would reduce risk to military assets, third party nations, or CONUS assets, for example, discovering a contagious disease or having low level chemical or radiological exposure symptoms appear in transit to/from the theatre increase risk to both current and future movement.

4S Category:
Sense

Operational Risk Management Guideline:
Commanders should not assume that they will have clear warning. Not all trigger events are created equal. Commanders cannot solely or primarily rely on intelligence triggers, detection device trigger events, or weapons trigger events to institute tactical level defensive measures that might spare his operational capability. This means that sentinel casualties are your most likely indicator of a CBRN event unless shielding was applied prior to an event.

Factors Contributing to Operational Risk:

- You may complicate your ability to operate inadvertently because you didn't know you had an event. For example, you moved contaminated or exposed assets because detection methods failed to detect the event, sentinel casualties appeared en route in transit to/from the theater.
- If sentinel casualties are your first indicator of a CBRN event, you already have an operational impact.
- Intelligence trigger events have not proven to be reliable, weapons trigger events (except for an obvious mushroom cloud or TBM explosion) are unlikely.
- Detection trigger events (except for medical surveillance and radiological detectors) are either unlikely to sense an event, do not detect down to dangerous levels or exposure, or have such high false positive rates as to be questionably useful for informing operational decision making.
- Medical surveillance may be a superior method for detecting biological events, and may be more useful than detectors in identifying chemical events in unprotected populations, and even for radiological events if contamination or exposure was not obvious.
- Commanders are unlikely to suspect, and therefore sample, for use of CBRN agents unless there was a large weapon event (TBM) in a CBRN threat area,
- Commanders risk operational impacts from a CBRN event if they do not have a multi-layered CBRN defense sensing plan and capabilities in place.
- Continuing operations as usual after a sentinel casualty trigger event risks future operations if a latent casualty occurs outside of the operational area.
- Sometimes you cannot determine whether people, equipment, facilities or areas have been contaminated or exposed to CBRN until days or weeks after exposure. Most contamination is not obvious, so you may have to base many of your operational decisions on clinical symptoms.
- Commanders will likely have to rely on medical surveillance in conjunction with epidemiology and contact tracing following a biological event to determine who has contracted or been exposed to a disease. They will also have to impose disease containment measures for biological events, which are very costly to operational capability because they reduce the number of personnel available for duty.

4S Category:

Sense

Operational Risk Management Guideline:
Commander should assume that a trigger event is an actual event until proven otherwise. Commanders should manage CBRN trigger events and ambiguous test results as actual CBRN events until testing confirms that no event has occurred.

Factors Contributing to Operational Risk:
- A trigger event may have as much impact on operations initially as an actual event does.
- Unsubstantiated trigger events can be very costly to operations, especially since detection devices can be prone to a high proportion of false positives. Shielding and sustaining strategies (especially disease containment measures) are costly to operations in both time and personnel. But continuing operations as usual after a trigger event without applying shielding strategies risks future operations if a latent casualty occurs outside of the operational area.
- SOF/terrorist nuclear events are unlikely because SOF/terrorists are unlikely to possess nuclear technology.
- SOF/terrorist chemical events are not likely to have significant operational impact due to the limited amount of agent SOF/terrorists can carry.

4S Category:
Sense

Operational Risk Management Guideline:
Commanders must understand which sensing methods they can use to identify operationally "safe" and clearance "safe."

Factors Contributing to Operational Risk:
- Commanders will attempt to identify which operational assets (personnel, equipment, facilities and areas) have been affected by the CBRN event before continuing military operations unless the failure to continue operations will result in the failure of the campaign.
- Using the correct method can increase operational capability by quickly assessing which assets can be used in operational or clearance areas.
- Commanders can generally use currently fielded detection devices to determine whether assets are contaminated beyond operationally "safe" levels after a chemical and radiological event because they can measure down to those levels. This may not apply to TICs, TIMs, or NTAs.

- Commanders should use currently fielded detection devices to determine either operationally or clearance "safe" levels for radiological events.
- Commanders should not use currently fielded detection devices to determine either operationally or clearance "safe" levels for biological events.
- Commanders cannot use currently fielded detection devices to determine clearance "safe" for chemical events since current fielded capabilities cannot measure down to "safe" clearance levels.
- Using the wrong equipment or methods can result in confusion and loss of operational capability as more testing will be required to determine the level of "safe" for the asset in question.

4S Category:
Sense

Operational Risk Management Guideline:
Commanders should understand when characterizing (especially quantifying) CBRN agents gains them operational capability.

Factors Contributing to Operational Risk:
- Few currently fielded detection capabilities can quantify CBRN hazards.
- We have reasonably good capability for characterizing radiological agents quickly.
- We have the ability to characterize a few broad categories of chemical agents quickly, but limited capability to distinguish specific agents.
- We have limited field means for characterizing biological agents quickly (less than two hours), and even then we do not know if the agent is a live pathogen (an operational threat) or a dead one (not an operational threat).
- We cannot reliably quantify chemical vapor hazards outside of a laboratory other than being above the thresholds for current detection capability.
- We can quantify radiological hazards for specific areas.
- We have no means to quantify chemical liquid hazards.
- We have no means to quantify biological hazards
- Operational capability is gained by quantifying chemical and

radiological hazards. Field detection devices can tell commanders when they are above "safe" thresholds for operating in a CBRN environment.

- No gain in operational capability gained by quantifying biological agents. Commanders should not expend valuable assets trying to quantify biological agents (exception: persistent biological pathogens such as spores, and then only upon the advice of subject matter experts).
- Operational capability can be lost to diversion of critical personnel or augmentees required for operations to useless sampling and testing.
- You may reflexively overreact and thus expend precious time and assets and exhaust scarce resources trying to gather information that may not be useful in operational decision making (e.g., the hazard area for biological events) or decontaminating when other options (weathering, hazard avoidance are more expedient.

4S Category:
Sense

Operational Risk Management Guideline:
Commanders should assume that an asset is exposed or contaminated if it comes in contact with another asset that has been exposed or contaminated with CBRN agent until proven otherwise.

Factors Contributing to Operational Risk:
This can be costly to operations since it renders assets unusable until they can be assessed for CBRN contamination. This status will change, however, returning assets to operations if they are "safe" for their intended use.

4S Category:
Sense

Operational Risk Management Guideline:
Commanders will make every effort to identify and track contaminated or exposed assets per NATO protocol. The record should also record what actions were used to attain "safe" standards.

Factors Contributing to Operational Risk:

• Tracking and monitoring of contaminated assets reduces the risk to personnel and other assets by marking what is known about the contamination so that proper shielding and sustainment measures can be applied.

4S Category:

Sense

Operational Risk Management Guideline:

Commanders cannot rely on currently fielded detectors to provide adequate advance warning of potential CBRN events.

Factors Contributing to Operational Risk:

• The lack of genuine stand-off detection capability for CBRN, limited point-detection capability for chemical and radiological/nuclear agents, and only very limited point-detection capability for biological agents means that there will likely be little or no warning of a CBRN event until after it has occurred, if at all. Consequently, operational capability will be at risk for exposure to or contamination by CBRN.

4S Category:

Shape

Operational Risk Management Guideline:

Commanders cannot rely on currently fielded detectors to provide adequate advance warning of potential CBRN events.

Factors Contributing to Operational Risk:

• The lack of genuine stand-off detection capability for CBRN, limited point-detection capability for chemical and radiological/nuclear agents, and only very limited point-detection capability for biological agents means that there will likely be little or no warning of a CBRN event until after it has occurred, if at all. Consequently, operational capability will be at risk for exposure to or contamination by CBRN.

4S Category:

Shape

Operational Risk Management Guideline:

The commander should understand how the limitations of shape capabilities impacts his ability to assess his CBRN threat, his vulnerabilities, and consequently, on how manage risk to his operations.

Factors Contributing to Operational Risk:

- While doctrine relies heavily on the commander's ability to shape the battle-space, the commander has limited shape capabilities for CBRN.
  - Limited HUMINT on adversary CBRN capabilities, intent, method, and willingness to employ CBRN against US military assets.
  - Limited understanding of the specific effects of many of the CBRN agents on operational capabilities
  - Limited understanding of the fragility of operational capabilities to the CBRN threat.

4S Category:

Shape

Operational Risk Management Guideline:

Commanders cannot identify hazard areas for chemical and biological events with any accuracy using modeling and simulation tools due to the complexity of conditions that affect the tools' outputs. Equipment can, however, determine the parameters of a radiological or nuclear event.

Factors Contributing to Operational Risk:

- This means that commanders should assume that chemical or biological events have contaminated or exposed much of his operational area, and that he must therefore treat his military assets as if contaminated or exposed until proven otherwise, which is very costly to operational capability.

4S Category:

Shape

Operational Risk Management Guideline:

Commanders must understand that surviving and operating in a CBRN environment requires more comprehensive planning and preparation than any other battlefield threat.

Factors Contributing to Operational Risk:

- CBRN is an unfamiliar and complex operating environment, slowing operational decision making down significantly due to questions the commander will likely ask and doubts or confusion about the advice he has been given.
- CBNR has an asymmetrical, widely varying and disproportionate impact on warfighting assets (personnel, equipment, facilities and areas). Many times these impacts cannot be measured with accuracy. This slows operations and operational planning significantly.

4S Category:

Shape

Operational Risk Management Guideline:

CBRN will create conditions that will fundamentally change the way commanders normally operate.

Factors Contributing to Operational Risk:

- Without comprehensive, advanced planning and preparation appropriate to the CBRN threat, commanders will not be able to adjust quickly enough to the CBRN environment to stay in the fight.
- Commanders must also decide in advance how far they are willing to push their campaign if the threat is credible or if there has been a CBRN event.
- Planning and preparation should support this decision.

4S Category:

Shape

Operational Risk Management Guideline:

Commanders should engage the international community, critical allies, and critical US governors early and frequently on CBRN issues to facilitate military operational capability if a CBRN event occurs.

Factors Contributing to Operational Risk:

- Reducing risks to military operations requires complex collaboration and coordination of all potentially affected by CBRN risks.

- Trust is necessary for the conduct of post-CBRN event actions of any type and cannot be established without a basis upon which to communicate.

4S Category:
Shape

Operational Risk Management Guideline:
Commanders should use public affairs to their advantage. Commanders should be as proactive as the need to maintain strategic advantage allows him with regard to the "CNN effect."

Factors Contributing to Operational Risk:
- Waiting until CNN reports the event on its international news service will have a negative impact on trust, and consequently, on operational capability.
- The public at large cannot easily understand the difference between operationally "safe" and clearance "safe," and having that debate on international television should be avoided.

4S Category:
Shape

Operational Risk Management Guideline:
Commanders should understand how political issues and perceptions (e.g., whether an event was deliberate or not) can complicate or interfere with US command level decision making.

Factors Contributing to Operational Risk:
- Because the standards are difficult for the public to understand, it is incumbent upon the political and military leadership to help shape the public's perception of the risks CBRN poses to them.

4S Category:
Shape

Operational Risk Management Guideline:
Commanders should establish who (governmental and nongovernmental host nation, international, US states) has final authority over their ability to execute military operations, and establish and normalize interaction with them.

Factors Contributing to Operational Risk:
- Commanders do not make operational or strategic decisions in a vacuum. Many times non-US legal authorities have final say over your ability to execute a particular operation. This will be particularly true for CBRN since it appears to carry greater risks to the general population than other battlefield risks.

4S Category:
Shape

Operational Risk Management Guideline:
Commanders should determine whether they will operate in a CBRN environment, and the level of risk they are willing to take if they decide to do so.

Factors Contributing to Operational Risk:
- Pre-determining the level of risk that the commander will accept to survive and operate will shape planning and preparation. These, in turn, are the cornerstones of operational capability.

4S Category:
Shape

Operational Risk Management Guideline:
Commanders should understand when shielding is an effective strategy for sustaining operational capability and when it interferes with it.

Factors Contributing to Operational Risk:
- Shielding may not be very effective for radiological or nuclear events due to the nature of radiation, thus it may negatively impact operational capability if unnecessary or ineffective.

- Hazard avoidance measures may be the most effective method for preventing or reducing the exposure of personnel, equipment, facilities, and areas to CBRN hazards as well as for reducing psychological effects caused by CBRN events.
- Disease containment measures (including medical prophylaxis) are the most effective methods for preventing disease once exposure or transmission of diseases has occurred, but are also very costly in terms of operational capability.
- Physical protection measures can be very effective against chemical agents if employed before exposure to threshold levels of chemical agents, but are costly to operational capability.
- Physical protection can be very effective against biological agents if applied before exposure to biological agents, but are costly to operational capability.
- Long periods in physical protection result in operational degrade due to its clumsiness, physical exhaustion or dehydration, impact on visual field, physical exhaustion, and the impact on morale.

4S Category:
Shield

Operational Risk Management Guideline:
Commanders should understand what tactical CBRN defense actions will best sustain operational capability (see CONOPS, above).

Factors Contributing to Operational Risk:
- It is important to apply defense actions in a methodical way to optimize operational capability.

4S Category:
Shield

Operational Risk Management Guideline:
Commanders should consider applying shielding (e.g., vaccination before personnel are sent to the operational area, prophylaxis, physical protection measures – IPE/PPE, COLPRO, SIP) in response to any credible CBRN trigger event.

Factors Contributing to Operational Risk:

- Commanders will identify operational assets which require shielding prior to operations due to their criticality to the operation or inability to sense in time to protect them following a CBRN trigger event.
- All shielding activities can have positive psychological, and consequently, positive operational effects. To remain effective, however, they need to be used judiciously. Multiple warnings to apply physical protection without confirmation of a CBRN event can result in pathological fearfulness or deadly apathy if an actual CBRN event occurs. Commanders will have to weigh the risk of raising multiple (ultimately) false alarms versus the risk of an actual CBRN event occurring.
- Shielding can also have negative psychological effects on unprotected Allies, combined forces and civilians that may reduce operational capability. But, conversely, it can have negative effects on adversaries that lack equipment, improving operational advantage.
- Commanders should understand that even protected personnel, equipment, facilities, and areas involved in chemical and biological events that are "safe" for clearance may be subject to particular scrutiny for operations requiring intertheater movement, thus slowing OPSTEMPO.

4S Category:
Shield

Operational Risk Management Guideline:
Commanders in the theater of operations will seek to operate only with assets that are shielded against CBRN, uncontaminated, unexposed, or operationally "safe." They will avoid assigning personnel to operate in or with such as well. Individual personnel should not be asked to perform missions in ways where their cumulative CBRN dose exceeds a potential casualty-causing threshold. Commanders will only consider violating this guideline if the failure to execute their mission will result in campaign failure. If such assignments must be made due to criticality of operations, they will apply shielding that will ensure that contamination or exposure does not exceed operationally safe standards.

Factors Contributing to Operational Risk:

• Commanders must ensure that personnel operate in "safe" areas, with "safe" equipment, and in "safe" facilities unless the operational imperative is so critical that the campaign would be lost. This goes one step beyond current guidance in insisting that commanders balance operational risk on the side of personnel if there is any balancing to be done.

4S Category:
Shield

Operational Risk Management Guideline:
Commanders will strenuously avoid contaminating or exposing strategic lift to CBRN. They will allow strategic lift to carry contaminated personnel or equipment only by exception and for compelling reasons; even then, they will avoid allowing more than a very small percentage of their strategic lift aircraft, ships, and personnel from becoming contaminated.

Factors Contributing to Operational Risk:

• Strategic lift assets are relatively rare and disproportionately expensive and difficult to replace quickly. Thus every effort will be made to avoid exposing them to or contaminating them with CBRN. This will retain maximum lift capability.

4S Category:
Shield

Operational Risk Management Guideline:
Commanders will seek to exclude personnel who cannot tolerate shielding actions for the length of the mission, who may contaminate or expose other assets to CBRN, or who are psychologically unfit from missions in CBRN environments due to the liability of not being able to complete the mission.

Factors Contributing to Operational Risk:

• Pilots with miosis, personnel with nausea and vomiting, personnel exposed to diseases who could become symptomatic within the duration of the mission, and all personnel exhibiting unacceptable levels of stress will likely degrade operational capability and are thus excluded from the mission.

4S Category:
Shield

Operational Risk Management Guideline:
Commanders should maintain a CBRN status for their AOR. This status will reflect CBRN threats, CBRN trigger events, and confirmed CBRN use. The baseline status should be "No CBRN use in the AOR," followed by "CBRN trigger event in the AOR," and "Confirmed CBRN event in the AOR" with detailed information on operational areas and assets affected by the event.

Factors Contributing to Operational Risk:
- Maintaining and upgrading the AOR level status will allow planners to anticipate changes in operational capability over the course of the mission, building efficiency into operational planning.

4S Category:
Sustain

Operational Risk Management Guideline:
Commanders will determine boundaries and authorities that can limit their operational decisions following a CBRN event.

Factors Contributing to Operational Risk:
- Lack of knowledge of host nation, international, third party nation, and US states' laws, regulations, statutes, and CBRN response plans may drastically alter the commander's ability to execute both his operational plan and his CBRN response plan.

4S Category:
Sustain

Operational Risk Management Guideline:
Commanders should understand the impacts of medical therapy on operational capability.

Factors Contributing to Operational Risk:
- There are two aspects of medical therapy that have operational impacts:
  - In diseases that have protracted recovery periods, return to duty will not be prompt.
  - Some disease effects are irreversible even if medical therapy is successful, and not all personnel will be able to return to the field.
- It can require substantial resources and personnel to conduct and this may impact personnel available for operations.

4S Category:
Sustain

Operational Risk Management Guideline:
Commanders should understand how decontamination can sustain or negatively impact his operational capability.

Factors Contributing to Operational Risk:
- Chemical decontamination is possible but often difficult and resource intensive. In spite of all efforts, you may not be able to reduce contamination to clearance levels. This can result in restricting equipment for use in the operational area only, or even abandoning equipment.
- Some equipment cannot be decontaminated due to the damage decontamination can do to the equipment (e.g., sensitive electronics, gaskets, plastics). Commanders can continue to use contaminated equipment that meets "safe" standards for operational areas, but some equipment will not meet those standards and cannot be used in operations.
- Verification of clearance standards for "safe" may require specialized equipment and personnel to conduct if science-based procedures for achieving "safe" standards for operational and clearance cannot be developed or validated.
- Decontamination is not generally needed for biological events except in the case of persistent agents. It may however, have a powerfully positive (but

immeasurable) psychological effect on personnel. Consequently, the commander will have to weigh the psychological benefits of decontamination following a biological event against the costs (e.g., personnel, time, resources) of decontamination.

- Decontamination often leaves residuals that, if sufficient, may directly interfere with operational capability if they must be remediated during wartime. These residuals may also indirectly interfere with operational capability by producing residual hazards or environmental impacts.

4S Category:
Sustain

Operational Risk Management Guideline:
Commanders will assure that during operations, all military assets conform to the operational standards applicable for the area in which they are operating or transiting.

Factors Contributing to Operational Risk:
- Failure to conform to the "safe" standards established by the operational or transit area may impact both current and future ability to conduct operations using that area due to loss of trust issues.

4S Category:
Sustain

Operational Risk Management Guideline:
Commanders will minimize the fraction of assets subject to clearance standards.

Factors Contributing to Operational Risk:
- Clearance verification can significantly slow the movement of those assets down significantly.

4S Category:
Sustain

Operational Risk Management Guideline:

Theater Commanders will not be able to determine whether contaminated or exposed assets can meet clearance standards for safe because they lack the sensing capability.

Factors Contributing to Operational Risk:

• Clearance standards have been intentionally set to levels that will ensure no effects on the general population, whether here in the United States or abroad. Consequently, commanders may have to relegate contaminated or exposed assets to operational area use only, abandon them, or rely on the ability of political leadership to negotiate other standards that allow the return of assets to an area outside of the operational area.

4S Category:

Sustain

Operational Risk Management Guideline:

Commanders will avoid sending strategic lift and related assets to operational areas that have been contaminated or exposed to CBRN, even if those areas are believed to have been mitigated to operationally "safe" levels.

Factors Contributing to Operational Risk:

• Commanders will make it a priority to keep strategic lift and related assets uncontaminated and unexposed, as the delays associated with achieving clearance standards could slow the logistics and force flow to unacceptable levels.

4S Category:

Sustain

Operational Risk Management Guideline:

Commanders should assume that areas outside the immediate operational area will require clearance "safe." The TRANSCOM Commander will determine "clearance safe" for each operational boundary (host nation, third party nation, international waters and airspace, operational staging areas, US states or territories) involved in strategic lift. While it is possible that authorities may relax their safety standards in order to facilitate US military operations, they will in no case be set higher than the operationally "safe" standards for US military operations. Moreover, the TRANSCOM Commander will apply a safety margin to operationally "safe" if required to move civilians and especially children or older people.

Factors Contributing to Operational Risk:
- Clearance "safe" always reduces operational capability because it is a strict requirement for contaminated and exposed assets and because it is difficult, if not impossible, to measure or assure that those levels have been met.
- The commander has the discretion to set transit levels for civilians and other nonmilitary personnel to levels less than "operationally safe" if leaving them in the contaminated or exposed area poses a greater risk to them.

4S Category:
Sustain

Operational Risk Management Guideline:
The TRANSCOM Commander will determine whether and how alternative clearance standards will be established and ascertained. If he cannot, US clearance "safe" standards will apply. If alternative standards can be ascertained, the TRANSCOM Commander will determine whether to allow strategic lift into these locations.

Factors Contributing to Operational Risk:
- The TRANSCOM commander has the discretion to adjust clearance "safe" standards, but he must, at the same time, identify the means by which he can verify that the levels he has established are attained. This may be more costly to operational timeline if he cannot establish the latter.

4S Category:
Sustain

Operational Risk Management Guideline:
Commanders must understand that CBRN will change the way they calculate and manage risk to operations.

Factors Contributing to Operational Risk:
- CBRN risk to operations is difficult to gauge because not all conditions are as objective as they are for conventional operations.
- Political factors due to the hazard CBRN carries to civilian populations in the host nation, staging areas, third party countries, international waters and airspace, and US states and territories will impact the commander's ability to conduct business as usual.

4S Category:
Sustain

Operational Risk Management Guideline:
The commander's own reactions to the event can have both negative and positive impacts on operational capability.

Factors Contributing to Operational Risk:
- In an effort to avoid risk, commanders may react more conservatively than required given the contamination and exposure standards, and thus degrade operations unnecessarily.
- Commanders may also inadvertently degrade operational capability by reacting too cavalierly (for example, by sending a contaminated aircraft back to the US and creating a political environment that makes it more difficult to get overflight clearances in the future) because you don't completely understand the potential risks.

4S Category:
Sustain

Operational Risk Management Guideline:

Commanders must understand how the vulnerability of a collocated host nation military, military dependents, or nearby civilian populations to a CBRN event may affect their ability to operate following an event.

Factors Contributing to Operational Risk:

- The presence of these populations in or near the operational area, host nation, staging areas, third party countries, international waters and air-space, and US states and territories must be included in your risk calculation to remain operational.
- Excluding or dismissing civilian concerns may be perceived poorly by political leadership and result in an unrecoverable loss of operational capability if they shut down air space, port access, or otherwise limit your access.

4S Category:

Sustain

Operational Risk Management Guideline:

Commanders may have to make difficult choices about the use of scarce assets and resources if they need to sustain their operational capability.

Factors Contributing to Operational Risk:

- The commander may have to address concerns or requests for protection or assistance from nonmilitary populations in order to sustain your operational capability. This is especially true if the commander has to use host nation resources (e.g., contractors, transportation vehicles, medical facilities, etc.) or transit through them to reach assets he needs to continue the fight.

4S Category:

Sustain

Operational Risk Management Guideline:

Commanders should transparently, accurately, and frequently report accurate CBRN events to establish US credibility.

Factors Contributing to Operational Risk:

- The US government should work with critical partner nations (those whose territories we may have to use for staging areas or transit areas) and US states to understand the standards that it has established for "operationally safe" and "clearance safe" prior to a CBRN event in order to ensure or facilitate operational capability.

4S Category:

Sustain

Operational Risk Management Guideline:

Commanders should anticipate how psychological impacts may impede or complicate operational capability.

Factors Contributing to Operational Risk:

- Military personnel are not immune from psychological impacts of events. Due to both its inherent and perceived risks, CBRN has the potential to induce a greater number of psychological casualties than other battlefield events.
- The worried well, psychological casualties, and absenteeism due to the presence of dependents in the operational area can reduce personnel available for operations and increase competition for assets required for operations.
- Military personnel may more likely to choose to protect their dependents if there is a CBRN event, increasing absenteeism that will have an impact on operational capability.

4S Category:

Sustain

Operational Risk Management Guideline:

Commanders must assure that critical resources required to attain "safe" are in place.

Factors Contributing to Operational Risk:

- A lack of access to those resources will reduce operational capability because the commander will not be able to attain "safe" for operational or clearance purposes. Even with adequate resources in place, commanders

may not be able to process down to the level of "safe" necessary to conduct their operational plans.
- Keeping or making military assets "safe" may be resource intensive. Commanders should:
  - Prioritize their need for such assets according to their threat assessments
  - Know the capabilities and limitations of the resources for attaining "operational safe" and "clearance safe"
  - Have adequate and appropriate resources in place, know who owns them (US military, host nation, allies), and know the willingness of others to contribute those resources
  - Extent is US military is willing to commit more resources if doing so puts other theaters or homeland at risk

4S Category:
Sustain

Operational Risk Management Guideline:
Commanders will apply the CONOPS to both inward and outward bound operational assets.

Factors Contributing to Operational Risk:
- While commanders normally think in terms of contaminating or exposing clean assets by exposing them to dirty assets from the operational area, the reverse is true as well. Commanders should consider bringing clean assets into a contaminated or exposed operational area or in contact with contaminated or exposed assets.
- In either case, with regard to military assets and operational capability, "operationally clean" standards will apply.

4S Category:
Sustain

▪ The Stafford Act

The Robert T. Stafford Disaster Relief and Emergency Assistance Act. The Stafford Act is the primary legal authority for Federal participation in domestic disaster relief. When incidents that are declared disasters or emergencies by the President occur, Federal support to states is delivered in accordance with relevant provisions of the Stafford Act. A governor may request the President to declare a major disaster or emergency if the governor finds that effective response to the event is beyond the combined response capabilities of the state and affected local governments. Based on the findings of a joint Federal-state-local preliminary damage assessment indicating the damages are of sufficient severity and magnitude to warrant assistance under the act, the President may issue a major disaster or emergency declaration. Federal assistance takes many forms — including the direct provision of goods and services, financial assistance (through insurance, grants, loans, and direct payments), and technical assistance — and can come from various sources. Under the NRP construct, DOD is designated a support agency for all emergency support functions (ESFs) and a cooperating agency for a number of NRP support and incident annexes. The ESFs serve as the primary operational-level mechanism to provide assistance to state, local, and tribal governments or to Federal departments and agencies conducting missions of primary Federal responsibility.

(Source: Joint Publication (JP) 3-41 Chemical, Biological, Radiological, Nuclear, and High-Yield Explosives Consequence Management)

Stafford Act Assistance. A Stafford Act incident is one in which state and local authorities declare a state of emergency and request federal assistance. This type of emergency is an incident for which the Stafford Act establishes programs and processes for the Federal government to provide major disaster and emergency assistance to states, local governments, tribal nations, individuals, and qualified private nonprofit organizations.

(1) The Robert T. Stafford Disaster Relief and Emergency Assistance Act authorizes the Federal government to establish programs and process-es for the Federal government to provide major disaster and emer-gency assistance to states, local governments, tribal nations, individu-als, and qualified private nonprofit organizations.

(2) In some circumstances, Stafford Act requests may originate from the state emergency operations center (EOC), FEMA RRCC, or the FEMA NRCC and pass directly to the Joint Director of Military Support (JDOMS) or the DOD Office of the Executive Secretary, rather than routing though a DCO. These RFAs are processed the same as non-Stafford Act requests, with JDOMS and the Department of Defense Operational Environment operational headquarters conducting parallel coordination and providing a recommendation to Assistant Secretary of Defense for Homeland Defense and Americas' Security Affairs (ASD[HD&ASA]) and the SecDef for approval or disapproval. In all these cases, the supported CCDR and the affected DCO must be noti-fied to limit redundant coordination of resources.

(Source: Joint Publication (JP) 3-28 Civil Support)

▪ Posse Comitatus Act

Posse Comitatus Act (Title 18 USC, Section 1385). This federal statute places strict limits on the use of federal military personnel for law enforcement. Enacted in 1878, the PCA prohibits the willful use of the US Army (and later, the US Air Force) to execute the laws, except as authorized by the Congress or the US Constitution. Although the PCA, by its terms, refers only to the Army and Air Force, DOD policy extends the prohibitions of the Act to US Navy and Marine Corps forces, as well. Specifically prohibited activities include: interdiction of a vehicle, vessel, aircraft, or similar activity; search and/or seizure; arrest, apprehension, "stop-and-frisk" detentions, and similar activities; and use of military personnel for surveillance or pursuit of individuals, or as undercover agents, informants, investigators, or interrogators.
(Source: Joint Publication (JP) 3-28 Civil Support)

Posse Comitatus Act (Title 18 USC, Section 1385). Under the PCA, active-duty Federal military personnel may not participate in law enforcement activities except as otherwise authorized by the Constitution or statute. However, Congress specifically authorized military forces to engage in law enforcement activities when dealing with emergency situations involving nuclear materials. See 18 USC 831 and DODD 5525.5.

(Source: Joint Publication (JP) 3-41 Chemical, Biological, Radiological, Nuclear, and High-Yield Explosives Consequence Management)

DODD 5525.5: DoD Cooperation with Civilian Law Enforcement Officials

E4.1.2. Permissible direct assistance. The following activities are not restricted by [the Posse Comitatus Act]:...

> E4.1.2.5.5.5. Assistance in the case of crimes involving nuclear materials. See 18 U.S.C. §831

18 U.S.C. § 831. Prohibited transactions involving nuclear materials

(d) The Attorney General may request assistance from the Secretary of Defense under chapter 18 of title 10 in the enforcement of this section and the Secretary of Defense may provide such assistance in accordance with chapter 18 of title 10, except that the Secretary of Defense may provide such assistance through any Department of Defense personnel.

(e)

(1) The Attorney General may also request assistance from the Secretary of Defense under this subsection in the enforcement of this section. Notwithstanding section 1385 of this title, the Secretary of Defense may, in accordance with other applicable law, provide such assistance to the Attorney General if—

(A) an emergency situation exists (as jointly determined by the Attorney General and the Secretary of Defense in their discretion); and

(B) the provision of such assistance will not adversely affect the military preparedness of the United States (as determined by the Secretary of Defense in such Secretary's discretion).

(2) As used in this subsection, the term "emergency situation" means a circumstance—

(A) that poses a serious threat to the interests of the United States; and

(B) in which—

(i) enforcement of the law would be seriously impaired if the assistance were not provided; and

(ii) civilian law enforcement personnel are not capable of enforcing the law.

(3) Assistance under this section may include—

(A) use of personnel of the Department of Defense to arrest persons and conduct searches and seizures with respect to violations of this section; and

(B) such other activity as is incidental to the enforcement of this section, or to the protection of persons or property from conduct that violates this section.

(4) The Secretary of Defense may require reimbursement as a condition of assistance under this section.

(5) The Attorney General may delegate the Attorney General's function under this subsection only to a Deputy, Associate, or Assistant Attorney General.

■ Logistics and CCMRF

Defense Support to Civil Authorities and Homeland Defense
Support Concepts

Logistics support for forces historically worked to replicate doctrinal support in an overseas theater, in a mature operational area and with assigned forces. The events of "9-11" and the subsequent Global War on Terrorism coupled with Hurricane Katrina's devastation in New Orleans have combined to force modifications in doctrine, force structure and America's expectations of the U. S. Military to respond to a Homeland event. The advent of the Department of Homeland Security and the National Response Plan further ensure a more deliberate, organized and planned Federal participation in both natural and man made disasters.

The rapid development of CONUS as an active theater is shown with USNORTHCOM's designation as a Combatant Commander and USARNORTH as the CONUS based Army Service Component Command. Effective 1 October 2008, USNORTHCOM will have assigned forces to conduct response in certain situations. All these events challenge many aspects of conventional doctrine, support structure and legal considerations for US Forces which are "deployed" within the United States.

A viable Concept of Support for CONUS operations has been developed. It is constantly being tested, modified and improved as unforeseen situations occur and as Defense Support to Civil Authorities (DSCA) and Homeland Defense (HLD) missions are studied and the Lessons Learned process applied.

The generic Support Concept is built around a USNORTHCOM designated Base Support Installation (BSI) becoming the primary logistics hub supporting deployed forces. When required, the BSI tailors existing BSI assets to support sustainment operations for deployed forces and, where gaps exist in capabilities, facilitate re-supply of common user logistics through other means such as contracting or request for forces. USNORTHCOM and USARNORTH work closely with the Army's Installation Management Command (IMCOM) and other Services installation leadership to insure all Service Installations understand their missions and are prepared for their potential role as a BSI.

U.S. Transportation Command (USTRANSCOM) will provide deployment and redeployment common-user air, land and sea transportation for forces engaged in civil support operation and provides aero-medical evacuation and tanker support as required. Additionally, USTRANSCOM is designated as DOD's distribution process owner, charged to integrate strategic and theater joint operations area (JOA) distribution. When requested by a federal agency and approved by SECDEF, USTRANSCOM may provide transportation support to non-DOD organizations.

Defense Logistics Agency (DLA) will provide logistics support for the missions of the military departments and the Unified Combatant Commands engaged in civil support operations. It also provides logistics support to other DOD components and certain federal agencies. DLA provides reuse, recycling, and disposal solutions, to include hazardous, non radioactive material disposal through its defense reutilization and marketing services.

Defense Contract Management Agency (DCMA) will provide contract administrative service support and assists USNORTHCOM and USJFLCC in developing contingency contracting packages as required

U.S. Army Material Command (AMC) through the Army Contracting Command (ACC) will coordinate with and execute contracting activities for supported commander and service components for supplies, services, and minor construction, which are not readily available through established supply channels during the execution of operations. AMC provides an Initial Response Team (IRT) for initial contracting support. ACC also coordinates with designated BSIs for sustainment operations if required.

AMC will provide supply support and containerized support packages such as shower units, toilets and water purification. Additionally, they may provide a wide range of support options using the LOGCAP concept.

DOD forces will be directed to deploy with essential logistics capabilities to operate self-sufficiently for transit from home station plus three (3) days supply of Common User Logistics (class I and III). After 3 days in the area, resources and support may be provided by the designated BSI, through purchases with unit's organic Government Purchase Card (GPC) or, if necessary, by the parent service component. The intent is to minimize any impact on local community resources. By OPORD, all deployed personnel will deploy with 30 days of supply (DOS) of personal demand items.

Services remain responsible for providing service unique logistics items, (e.g. uniforms, special equipment maintenance support and service specific repair parts) to their deployed forces. Units are required to maintain accountable records for all supplies requested, received and issued during the period of deployment. Requisition Project Codes will be published when received by JCS J4 in the OPORD or FRAGO.

Each DSCA and HLD mission will be different. As DOD forces are committed, a detailed Concept of Support will be created after analysis of the disaster area. Factors such as the disaster distance from a BSI, expected length of stay by DOD Forces, capability of the area to sustain DOD forces while continuing to support the civilian population as well as the assigned forces are critical factors and must be considered in the disaster specific support concept.

▪ Glossary

PART 1 — ABBREVIATIONS

AAR	After Action Report
AC	Active Component
ACERT	Army Contaminated Equipment Retrograde Team
ADVON	Advance Element
AFBAT	Air Force Biological Augmentation Team
AFCAT	Air Force Chemical Assessment Team
AFME	Armed Forces Medical Examiner
AFMS	Air Force Medical Service
AFNORTH	Air Forces, United States Northern Command
AFRAT	Air Force Radiation Assessment Team
AFRC	Air Force Reserve Command
AFTAC	Air Force Technical Applications Center
AIT	Aeromedical Isolation Team
ALCOM	Alaskan Command
AO	Area of Operations
AOI	Area of Interest
AOR	Area of Responsibility
APOD	Aerial Port of Debarkation
APOE	Aerial Port of Embarkation
ARNG	Army National Guard
ARNORTH	Army Forces, United States Northern Command
ASD	Assistant to the Secretary of Defense
ASD(HD)	Assistant to the Secretary of Defense for Homeland Defense
AT	Anti-Terrorism
AT/FP	Anti-Terrorism/Force Protection
BIDS	Biological Integrated Detection System
BEAR	Base Expeditionary Airfield Resources
BPT	Be Prepared To
BSI	Base Support Installation
C2	Command and Control
C3	Command, Control and Communications

C4	Command, Control, Communications and Computers
C4ISR	Command, Control, Communications, Computers, Intelligence, Surveillance and Reconnaissance
CA	Civil Affairs
CAE	Commander's Assessment Element
CAISE	Civil Authority Information Support Element
CBAD	Chemical/Biological Applications Division
CBRNE	Chemical, Biological, Radiological, Nuclear and High-Yield Explosives
CBRNE-CE	Chemical Biological-Radiological Nuclear and High Yield Explosives – Coordination Element
CBIRF	Chemical Biological Incident Response Force
CCIR	Commander's Critical Information Requirements
CCMRF	CBRNE CM Response Force
CCs/S/A	Combatant Commanders, Services, Agencies
CERFP	CBRNE Enhanced Response Force Packages
CDRAFNORTH	Commander, Air Force North
CDRARNORTH	Commander, Army North
CDRMARFORNORTH	Commander, Marine Forces North
CDRNORAD	Commander, North American Aerospace Defense Command
CDRUSNORTHCOM	Commander, United States Northern Command
CDRUSJFCOM	Commander, United States Joint Forces Command
CDRJTF-AK	Commander, Joint Task Force–Alaska
CDRJTF-CS	Commander, Joint Task Force–Civil Support
CDRJTF-NCR	Commander, Joint Task Force–National Capitol Region
CDRUSPACOM	Commander, United States Pacific Command
CDRUSSOCOM	Commander, United States Special Operations Command
CDRUSSOUTHCOM	Commander, United States Southern Command
CDRUSSTRATCOM	Commander, United States Strategic Command
CDRUSTRANSCOM	Commander, United States Transportation Command
CERT	Computer Emergency Response Team
CFFC	Commander, Fleet Forces Command
CI	Counterintelligence
CIA	Central Intelligence Agency

CIAO	Critical Infrastructure Assurance Office
CIFC	Combined Intelligence and Fusion Center
CIP	Critical Infrastructure Protection
CIS	Catastrophic Incident Supplement
CISO	Counterintelligence Staff Office
CJCS	Chairman, Joint Chiefs of Staff
CJTF	Commander Joint Task Force
CM	Consequence Management
CNA	Computer Network Attack
CND	Computer Network Defense
CNE	Computer Network Exploitation
CNO	Computer Network Operations
COA	Course of Action
COCOM	Combatant Command
COG	Centers of Gravity, Current Operations Group
COMCAM	Combat Camera
COMPUSEC	Computer Security
COMSEC	Communications Security
CONEMP	Concept of Employment
CONEX	Concept of Execution
CONOPS	Concept of Operations
CONPLAN	Concept Plan
CONUS	Continental United States
COOP	Continuity of Operations Plan
COP	Common Operational Picture
CPG	Contingency Planning Guidance
CRPL	CBRNE Response Posture Level
CS	Civil Support
CSS	Central Security Service, Combat Service Support
CT	Counterterrorism
DCE	Defense Coordinating Element
DCO	Defense Coordinating Officer
DCMA	Defense Contract Management Agency
DECON	Decontamination

DEPORD	Deployment Order
DHHS	Department of Health and Human Services
DHS	Department of Homeland Security
DIA	Defense Intelligence Agency
DIB	Defense Industrial Base
DIRLAUTH	Direct Liaison Authorized
DISA	Defense Information Systems Agency
DLA	Defense Logistics Agency
DOD	Department of Defense
DODD	Department of Defense Directive
DODI	Department of Defense Instruction
DOE	Department of Energy
DOJ	Department of Justice
DOS	Department of State
DOS	Days of Supply
DPG	Defense Planning Guidance
DSCA	Defense Support of Civil Authorities
DTRA	Defense Threat Reduction Agency
DTRG	Defense Technical Response Group
EEI	Essential Elements of Information
EOD	Explosive ordnance Disposal
EPA	Environmental Protection Agency
ESF	Emergency Support Function
EXORD	Execute Order
FEMA	Federal Emergency Management Agency
FFC	Fleet Forces Command
FOB	Forward Operating Base
FP	Force Protection
FPCON	Force Protection Conditions
FPO	Force Package Option
FUNCPLAN	Functional Plans
GCC	Geographic Combatant Commander
GEOINT	Geospatial Intelligence
GIG	Global Information Grid

GNO	Global Network Operation
GTN	Global Transportation Network
GWOT	Global War on Terrorism
HAZMAT	Hazardous Material
HD	Homeland Defense
HLS	Homeland Security
HPAC	Hazard Prediction and Assessment Capability
HSPD	Homeland Security Presidential Directive
IA	Information Assurance
IAW	In Accordance With
IC	Interagency Coordination
ICW	In Coordination With
IED	Improvised Explosive Device
IGO	Intergovernmental Organizations
IMINT	Imagery Intelligence
INFOCON	Information Operations Condition
INFOSEC	Information Security
IO	Information Operations
IOC	Initial Operational Capability
IOTC	Information Operations Technology Center
ISAC	Information Sharing and Analysis Center
ISO	In Support Of
ISR	Intelligence, Surveillance and Reconaissance
ISSA	Inter-service Support Agreement
ITA	Initial Threat Availability
ITV	In-Transit Visibility
JDOMS	Joint Director of Military Support
JFACC	Joint Force Air Component Commander
JFHQ	Joint Force Headquarters
JFLCC	Joint Force Land Component Commander
JFMCC	Joint Force Maritime Component Commander
JFO	Joint Field Office
JFUB	Joint Facilities Utilization Board
JIACG	Joint Interagency Coordination Group

JIATF	Joint Interagency Task Force
JMC	Joint Movement Center
JOA	Joint Operations Area
JOC	Joint Operation Center
JOPES	Joint Operations and Planning Execution System
JPAC	Joint Planning Augmentation Cell
JTAC	Joint Technical Augmentation Cell
JPO-STC	Joint Program Office for Special Technical Countermeasures
JRSOI	Joint Reception, Staging, Onward movement, and Integration
JS	Joint Staff
JSCP	Joint Strategic Capabilities Plan
JSOA	Joint Special Operations Area
JTAV	Joint Total Asset Visibility
JTF	Joint Task Force
LANTAREA	Atlantic Area (U.S. Coast Guard)
LEA	Law Enforcement Agency
LECIC	Law Enforcement and Counterintelligence Center (DOD)
LNO	Liaison Officer
LOC	Logistics Operations Center
LRC	Logistics Readiness Center
MA	Mission Assignment
MARFORNORTH	Marine Corps Forces, United States Northern Command
MCBAT	Medical Chemical Biological Advisory Team
MCT	Movement Control Team
METOC	Meteorological and Oceanographic
MFDO	Military Flexible Deterrent Option
MOA	Memoranda of Agreement
MOU	Memoranda of Understanding
MTF	Medical Treatment Facility
NCP	National Contingency Plan
NCR	National Capital Region
NG	National Guard

NG CERFP	National Guard CBRNE Enhanced Response Force Package
NGA	National Geospatial-Intelligence Agency
NGB	National Guard Bureau
NGO	Nongovernmental Organization
NIPC	National Infrastructure Protection Center
NIPRNET	Non-Secure Internet Protocol Router Network
NIST	National Institute of Standards and Technology
NLW/NLC	Non-lethal Weapons/Non-lethal Capabilities
NMCC	National Military Command Center
NOC	National Operations Center (Formerly Homeland Security Operations Center (HSOC)
NORAD	North American Aerospace Defense Command
NRF	National Response Framework
NSA	National Security Agency
NSC	National Security Council
NSPD	National Security Presidential Directive
NSSE	National Special Security Event
NIMS	National Incident Management System
OA	Operational Area
OASD	Office of the Assistant Secretary of Defense
OGA	Other Government Agency
ONR	Office of Naval Research
OPCON	Operational Control
OPLAN	Operation Plan
OPSEC	Operations Security
OSD	Office of the Secretary of Defense
PA	Public Affairs
PAG	Public Affairs Guidance
PCA	Posse Comitatus Act
PIR	Priority Information Requirement
PLANORD	Planning Order
POC	Point of Contact
POL	Petroleum, Oils, and Lubricants

POTUS	President of the United States
PVO	Private Volunteer Organizations
QRF	Quick Reaction Force
RADCON	Radiological Control
RAMT	Radiological Advisory Medical Team
RC	Reserve Component
RDD	Radiation Dispersal Device
RECON	Reconnaissance
REPLO	Regional Emergency Preparedness Liaison Officer
RFA	Request for Assistance
RFF	Request for Forces
RRCC	Regional Response Coordination Center
RRF	Ready Reserve Force
RSC	Regional Service Center
RUF	Rules for the Use of Force
SAAM	Special Assignment Airlift Mission
SAC	Situational Awareness Center
SecDef	Secretary of Defense
SEPLO	State Emergency Preparedness Liaison Officer
SGS	Strategic Guidance Statement
SIPRNET	Secure Internet Protocol Router Network
SJFHQ-N	Standing Joint Force Headquarters–North
SMART	Special Medical Augmentation Response Team
SPG	Strategic Planning Guidance
SPOE	Sea Port of Embarkation
SPOD	Sea Port of Debarkation
SRUF	Standing Rules for the Use of Force
TACON	Tactical Control
TAG	The Adjutant General
TBD	To Be Determined
TBP	To Be Published
TEU	Technical Escort Unit
TPFDD	Time-Phased Force and Deployment Data
TPFDDL	Time-Phased Force and Deployment Data List

TS	Top Secret
TSA	Transportation Security Agency
TSCP	Theater Security Cooperation Plan
TTIC	Terrorist Threat Integration Center
TTP	Tactics, Techniques and Procedures
U	UNCLASSIFIED
UCP	Unified Command Plan
UN	United Nations
US	United States
USACE	United States Corps of Engineers
USC	United States Code
USCG	United Stated Coast Guard
USG	United States Government
USGS	United States Geological Survey
USJFCOM	United States Joint Forces Command
USNORTHCOM	United States Northern Command
USPACOM	United State Pacific Command
USSOCOM	United States Special Operations Command
USSOUTHCOM	United States Southern Command
USSTRATCOM	United States Strategic Command
USTRANSCOM	United States Transportation Command
WARNORD	Warning Order
WMD	Weapons of Mass Destruction
WMD-CST	Weapons of Mass Destruction–Civil Support Teams

PART 2 — DEFINITIONS

Antiterrorism: Defensive measures used to reduce the vulnerability of individuals and property to terrorist acts, to include limited response and containment by local military forces. (JP 3-07.2)

Area of responsibility (AOR): The geographical area associated with a combatant command within which a combatant commander has authority to plan and conduct operations. (JP 1-02)

Base Support Installation (BSI): A Department of Defense service or agency installation within the United States, its territories, or possessions tasked to serve as a base for military forces engaged in either homeland defense or defense support to civil authorities operations. Provides general support logistic and administrative support to military forces. (JP 3-41.)

Chemical, biological, radiological, nuclear and high-yield explosives (CBRNE): Emergencies resulting from the deliberate or unintentional release of nuclear, biological, radiological or toxic poisonous chemical materials, or the detonation of a high yield explosive. (JP 1-02)

Chemical, Biological, Radiological, Nuclear, and High-Yield Explosives Consequence Management (CBRNE-CM): The consequence management activities for all deliberate and inadvertent releases of chemical, biological, radiological, nuclear, and high-yield explosives that are undertaken when directed or authorized by the President. (JP 3-41)

Civil Authorities: Those elected and appointed officers and employees who constitute the Government of the United States, of the 50 states, the District of Columbia, the Commonwealth of Puerto Rico, United States possessions and territories and political subdivisions thereof. (JP 1-02)

Civil Support (CS): Department of Defense support to US civil authorities for domestic emergencies, and for designated law enforcement and other activities (JP 1-02).

Command and Control (C2): The exercise of authority and direction by a properly designated commander over assigned and attached forces in the accomplishment of the mission. Command and control functions are performed through an arrangement of personnel, equipment, communications, facilities, and procedures employed by a commander in planning, directing, coordinating, and controlling forces and operations in the accomplishment of the mission. (JP 1-02)

Commander's Critical Information Requirements (CCIR): A comprehensive list of information requirements identified by the commander as being critical in facilitating timely information management and the decision-making process that affect successful mission accomplishment. The two key subcomponents are critical friendly force information and priority intelligence requirements. (JP 1-02)

Critical Infrastructure: Systems and assets, whether physical or virtual, that are so vital to the United States that the incapacity or destruction of such systems and assets would have a debilitating impact on security, national economic security, national public health or safety, or any combination of those matters.

Critical Infrastructure Protection (CIP): The identification, assessment, and security enhancement of physical and cyber assets essential to the orderly functioning of the government, economy, domestic activities and for the mobilization, deployment, employment, sustainment, and redeployment of U.S. military operations. The primary responsibility for the protection of private and state property lies with private enterprise, and local and state authorities. DOD assets will only be utilized when requested by state authorities and approved by SecDef. Protection of civil infrastructure is a civilian responsibility led by Department of Homeland Security (DHS). DOD's responsibility is to identify and coordinate protection of critical infrastructure necessary to execute the national military strategy.

Computer Network Attack (CNA): Operations to disrupt, deny, degrade, or destroy information resident in computers and computer networks, or the computers and networks themselves. Electronic attack (EA) can be used against a computer, but CNA relies on the data stream to execute the attack while EA relies on the electromagnetic spectrum. (JP 1-02)

Computer Network Defense (CND): Measures taken to protect and defend information, computers, and networks from disruption, denial, degradation or destruction. (JP 1-02)

Computer Network Operations (CNO): Defensive, offensive, and exploitation actions and operations conducted to ensure access to information, information systems, and networks; acquire intelligence and vulnerability information form adversary systems; and, when directed, deny an adversary access and use of their information and information systems. (DODD 3600.1)

Computer Network Exploitation (CNE): Activities by foreign intelligence collection entities involving intrusion into DOD computers and computer networks of the Global Information Grid (GIG). Some foreign intelligence and security services are using rapidly evolving technologies and methods to gain access to sensitive information by penetrating computer networks and their attached information systems. (DODD 3600.1)

Computer security (COMPSEC): A field of computer science concerned with the control of risks related to computer use. The means traditionally taken to realize this objective is to attempt to create a trusted and secure computing platform, designed so that agents (users or programs) can only perform actions that have been allowed. This involves specifying and implementing a security policy. The actions in question can be reduced to operations of access, modification and deletion. Computer security can be seen as a subfield of security engineering, which looks at broader security issues in addition to computer security.

Communications Security (COMSEC): Measures and controls taken to deny unauthorized persons information derived from telecommunications and ensure the authenticity of such telecommunications and ensure the authenticity of such telecommunications. Communications security includes crypto security, transmission security, emission security, traffic flow security, and physical security of COMSEC material.

Consequence Management (CM): Actions taken to maintain or restore essential services and manage and mitigate problems resulting from disasters and catastrophes, including natural, manmade, or terrorist incidents.

Continuity of Operations (COOP): The degree or state of being continuous in the conduct of functions, tasks, or duties necessary to accomplish a military action or mission in carrying out the national military strategy. It includes the functions and duties of the commander, as well as the supporting functions and duties performed by the staff and others acting under the authority and direction of the commander. (JP 1-02)

Common Operational Picture (COP): A single identical display of relevant information shared by more than one command. A common operational picture facilitates collaborative planning and assists all echelons to achieve situational awareness. (JP 1-02)

Counterterrorism (CT): Offensive measures taken to prevent, deter and respond to terrorism. (JP 1-02)

Course of Action (COA): Any sequence of activities that an individual or unit may follow. A product of the Joint Operation Planning and Execution System concept development phase. (JP 1-02)

Decontamination: The process of making any person, object, or area safe by absorbing, destroying, neutralizing, making harmless, or removing chemical or biological agents, or by removing radioactive material clinging to or around it. (JP 1-02)

Defense Coordinating Officer (DCO): The Department of Defense on-scene representative who coordinates defense support of civil authorities requirements with the Federal Coordinating Officer (FCO), or his or her designated representative. (JP 1-02.)

Defense Industrial Base (DIB): The DIB consists of DOD product and service providers. Many services and products are essential to mobilize, deploy, and sustain military operations; these services and products constitute assets for the DOD.

Defense Information Systems Agency (DISA): Combat support agency of the United States Department of Defense (DoD) responsible for planning, developing, fielding, operating and supporting command, control, communications and information systems that serve the needs of the President, the Secretary of Defense, the

Joint Chiefs of Staff, the Combatant commanders, and other Department of Defense components under all conditions of peace and war.

Defense Support of Civil Authorities (DSCA): DOD support, including Federal military forces, the Department's career civilian and contractor personnel, and DOD agency and component assets, for domestic emergencies and for designated law enforcement and other activities. The DOD provides defense support of civil authorities when directed to do so by the President or SecDef. (DODD 3025.dd (draft)

Emergency Support Functions (ESF): A grouping of government and certain private-sector capabilities into an organizational structure to provide the support, resources, program implementation, and services that are most likely to be needed to save lives, protect property and the environment, restore essential services and critical infrastructure, and help victims and communities return to normal, when feasible, following domestic incidents of domestic emergency, disaster, or catastrophe. The emergency support functions serve as the primary operational-level mechanism to provide assistance to state, local, and tribal governments or to Federal departments and agencies conducting missions of primary Federal responsibility.

First Responder: Local and non-governmental police, fire, and emergency personnel who in the early stages of an incident are responsible for the protection and preservation of life, property, evidence, and the environment. (NRP)

Force Protection: Actions taken to prevent or mitigate hostile actions against Department of Defense personnel (to include family members), resources, facilities, and critical information. These actions conserve the force's fighting potential so it can be applied at the decisive time and place and incorporates the coordinated and synchronized offensive and defensive measures to enable the effective employment of the joint force while degrading opportunities for the enemy. Force Protection does not include actions to defeat the enemy or protect against accidents, weather, or disease.

Force Protection Condition (FPCON): A Chairman of the Joint Chiefs of Staff approved program standardizing the Military Services' identification of and recommended responses to terrorist threats against US personnel and facilities. This program facilitates inter-Service coordination and support for antiterrorism activities.

Foreign Consequence Management (FCM): Assistance provided by the United States Government to a host nation to mitigate the effects of a deliberate or inadvertent chemical, biological, radiological, nuclear, or high-yield explosives attack or event and restore essential government services. (JP 3-41)

Global Information Grid (GIG): The globally interconnected, end-to-end set of information capabilities, associated processes and personnel for collecting, processing, storing, disseminating and managing information on demand to warfighters, policy makers, and support personnel. The GIG includes all owned and leased communications and computing systems and services, software (including applications), data, security services and other associated services necessary to achieve information superiority. It also includes National Security Systems as defined in section 5142 of the Clinger-Cohen Act of 1996. The GIG supports all Department of Defense (DOD), National Security, and related intelligence community missions and functions (strategic, operational, tactical and business), in war and in peace. The GIG provides capabilities from all operating locations (bases, posts, camps, stations, facilities, mobile platforms and deployed sites). The GIG provides interfaces to coalition, allied, and non-DOD users and systems. (JP 1-02)

Global Network Operations: Military operations which are responsible for providing global satellite communication systems status; maintaining global situational awareness to include each combatant commander's planned and current operations as well as contingency plans; supporting radio frequency interference resolution management supporting satellite anomaly resolution and management; facilitating satellite communications interference to the defense information infrastructure; and managing the regional satellite communications support centers.

Homeland: The United States. (See Homeland Security Act of 2002)

Homeland Defense (HD): The ability to protect U.S. sovereignty, territory, domestic population, and critical defense infrastructure against external threats and aggression, or other threats as directed by the President.

Homeland Security (HLS): Defined by the National Strategy for Homeland Security as a concerted national effort to prevent terrorist attacks within the United States, reduce America's vulnerability to terrorism, minimize damage and recover from attacks that do occur. (Upon approval of JP 3-26, Joint Doctrine for Homeland Security, this term and its definition will be included in JP 1-02).

Incident Management (InM): All actions taken to prepare for, prevent, respond to, or recover from any event impacting lives or property. It includes pre-event, during, and post-event activities. It can be associated with attack, natural, or man-made situations involving disasters or other catastrophic occurrences. It includes military assistance to civil authorities (MACA), military assistance during civil disturbances (MACDIS), and military assistance to law enforcement agencies programs under the umbrella of Defense Support of Civil Authorities (DSCA). It includes both domestic and foreign support operations. It includes humanitarian aid and relief missions. Actions include measures to protect public health and safety, restore essential governmental services, and provide emergency relief to governments, businesses, and individuals affected by the incident. (JP 3-41)

Information Assurance (IA): is the science of managing the risks to information assets. More specifically, IA practioners seek to protect the confidentiality, integrity and availability of networking services and data; whether the data is in storage, processing or transit, and whether the data and services are threatened by malice or accident. Information Assurance is closely related to information security and the terms are sometimes used interchangeably; however, IA's broader connotation also includes reliability and emphasizes strategic risk management over tools and tactics. In additional to defending against malicious hackers and viruses, IA includes other corporate governance issues such as privacy, compliance, audits, business continuity, and disaster recovery.

Information Operations (IO): Actions taken to affect adversary information and information systems while defending one's own information and information systems. (JP 1-02)

Information Operations Condition (INFOCON): Threat level system in the United States similar to that of Force Protection (FPCON). INFOCON is a defense system based primarily on the status of information systems and is a method use by the military to defense against a computer network attack. There are five levels of INFOCON, which recently changed to more closely correlate to DEFCON levels:

— **INFOCON 5** describes a situation where there is no apparent terrorist activity against computer networks. Operational performance of all information systems is monitored and passwords systems are used as a layer of protection.

— **INFOCON 4** describes an increased risk of attack. Increased monitoring of all network activities is mandated and all Department of Defense end users must make sure their systems are secure. Internet usage may be restricted to government sites only and backing up files to removable media is ideal.

— **INFOCON 3** describes when a risk has been identified. Security review on important on important systems is a priority and the Computer Network defense system's alertness is increased. All unclassified dial up connections are disconnected.

— **INFOCON 2** describes when an attack has taken place but the Computer Network Defense system is not at its highest alertness. Non-essential networks may be taken offline, and alternate methods of communications may be implemented.

— **INFOCON 1** describes when attacks are taking place and the Computer Network Defense system is at maximum alertness. Any compromised systems are isolated from the rest of the network.

Information security or sometimes Information Systems Security (INFOSEC): Deals with several different "trust" aspects of information and its protection. Another similar term is Information Assurance (IA) but INFOSEC is a subset of IA. Information security is not confined to computer systems, nor to information in an electronic or machine readable form. It applies to all aspects of safeguarding or protecting information or data, in whatever form or media.

Information warfare: Is the use and management of information in pursuit of a competitive advantage over an opponent. Information warfare may involve collection of tactical information, assurance that one's own information is valid, spreading of propaganda or disinformation among the enemy, undermining the quality of opposing force information and denial of information collection opportunities to opposing forces.

Joint Operations Area (JOA): An area of land, sea, and airspace, defined by a geographic combatant commander or subordinate unified commander, in which a joint force commander (normally a joint task force commander) conducts military operations to accomplish a specific mission. Joint operations areas are particularly useful when operations are limited in scope and geographic area or when operations are to be conducted on the boundaries between theaters. (JP 1-02)

Joint Planning Augmentation Cell (JPAC): The JPAC basic package consists of a four-member team led by an O-4/O-5 Team Chief. The other JPAC members are: an NBC/Hazardous Material (HAZMAT) Planner, Logistics Planner and Medical Planner. Based on the situation and requirements of the supported JTF, more JPAC members may be required and will be provided as appropriate. Critical planning expertise such as intelligence planning/products will be provided through the Joint Planning Group (JPG) and or Joint Planning Group (JPG) via reach-back support. Typically, the core JPAC membership will reside within the supporting, functional directorates. JPACs are specifically tailored or expanded to fit the needs of the supported organization or incident type. Additional members of a JPAC may include a Communications Planner/Technical Expert; J1 Personnel Planner; a Joint Operation Planning and Execution System (JOPES) planner; Mortuary Affairs Planner; Public Affairs Officer (PAO); Judge Advocate General (JAG); an Interagency Liaison Officer (LNO); or a J3 OPS representative. The JTF-CS J5 will staff the JPACs with SME augmentation provided by the directors and is responsible for training and keeping the JPACs proficient through internal and external training opportunities as well as participation in NSSEs as appropriate.

Joint Reception, Staging, Onward Movement, and Integration (JRSOI): A phase of joint force projection occurring in the operational area. This phase comprises the essential processes required to transition arriving personnel, equipment, and materiel into forces capable of meeting operational requirements. (JP 1-02)

Law Enforcement Agency (LEA): Any of a number of agencies (outside the Department of Defense) chartered and empowered to enforce US laws in the following jurisdictions: the United States, a state (or political division) of the United States, a territory or possession (or political subdivision) of the United States, or within the borders of a host nation. (JP 1-02)

Military Flexible Deterrent Option (MFDO): A planning construct intended to facilitate early decision by laying out a wide-range of interrelated response paths that begin with deterrent-oriented options carefully tailored to send the right signal. The flexible deterrent option is the means by which the various deterrent options available to a commander (such as economic, diplomatic, political, and military measures) are implemented into the planning process. (JP 1-02)

Mission Assignment (MA): The means by which the by Department of Homeland Security/Federal Emergency Management Agency provides and assigns federal support upon declaration of a major disaster or emergency as defined in the Stafford Act. It orders the mobilization of immediate, short-term emergency response assistance when an applicable state or local government is overwhelmed by the event and lacks the capability to perform, or contract for, the necessary work. Note: Department of Defense accepts all Federal Emergency Management Agency mission assignments as requests for assistance. These requests for assistance only become Department of Defense mission assignments once they have been vetted through the Office of the Assistant Secretary of Defense (Homeland Defense) and the Joint Director of Military Support and have been approved by the Secretary of Defense. (JP 3- 41).

Mission Assurance: The ability to ensure that assigned tasks or duties can be performed in accordance with the intended purpose or plan. Mission Assurance-such as force protection; antiterrorism; critical infrastructure protection; information assurance; DOD continuity operation; chemical, biological, radiological, nuclear, and high-explosive defense; and installation preparedness-to create the synergistic effect required for DOD to mobilize, deploy, support, and sustain military operations throughout the continuum of operations.

National Contingency Plan (NCP): The purpose of the National Oil and Hazardous Substances Pollution Contingency Plan (NCP) is to provide the organizational structure and procedures for preparing for and responding to discharges of oil and releases of hazardous substances, pollutants, and contaminants. (40 CFR Part 300-399).

National Operations Center (NOC): The NOC is the primary national hub for domestic incident management operational coordination and situational awareness. The NOC is a standing 24/7 interagency organization fusing law enforcement, national intelligence, emergency response, and private-sector reporting. The NOC facilitates homeland security information-sharing and operational coordination with other Federal, State, local, tribal, and nongovernmental EOCs.

National Special Security Events (NSSE): Special events of such national significance that require greater Federal visibility.

Nongovernmental Organizations (NGO): Transnational organizations of private citizens that maintain a consultative status with the Economic and Social Council of the United Nations. Nongovernmental organizations may be professional associations, foundations, multinational businesses, or simply groups with a common interest in humanitarian assistance activities (development and relief). (JP 3-31)

Ready Reserve Force (RRF): A force composed of ships acquired by the Maritime Administration (MARAD) with Navy funding and newer ships acquired by the MARAD for the National Defense Reserve Fleet (NDRF). Although part of the NDRF, ships of the Ready Reserve Force are maintained in a higher state of readiness and can be made available without mobilization or congressionally declared state of emergency.

Rules for the Use of Force (RUF): Directives issued to guide United States forces on the use of force during civil support operations. These directives may take the form of mission execute orders, deployment orders, memoranda of agreement, or plans. (Upon approval of JP 3-26, Joint Doctrine for Homeland Security, this term and its definition will be included in JP 1-02).

State: Any state of the United States, the District of Columbia, the Commonwealth of Puerto Rico, the Virgin Islands, Guam, American Samoa, the Commonwealth of the Northern Mariana Islands, and any possession of the United States. (Homeland Security Act of 2002)

Supported Commander: The commander having the primary responsibility for all aspects of a task assigned by the Joint Strategic Capabilities Plan or other joint operation planning authority. The commander who receives assistance from another commander's force or capabilities and who is responsible for ensuring that the supporting commander understands the assistance required. (JP 1-02)

Supporting Commander: A commander who provides augmentation forces or other support to a supported commander or who develops a supporting plan. Includes the designated combatant commands and Defense agencies as appropriate. See also supported commander. (JP 1-02)

Terrorism: The calculated use of unlawful violence or threat of unlawful violence to inculcate fear; intended to coerce or to intimidate governments or societies in the pursuit of goals that are generally political, religious, or ideological. (JP 1-02)

Threat analysis: In antiterrorism, a continual process of compiling and examining all available information concerning potential terrorist activities by terrorist groups which could target a facility.

Weapons of Mass Destruction (WMD): Weapons that are capable of a high order of destruction and/or being used in such a manner as to destroy large numbers of people. Weapons of Mass Destruction can be high explosives or nuclear, biological, chemical and radiological weapons, but exclude the means of transporting or propelling them where such means is a separable and divisible part of the weapon. (JP 1-02)

Weapons of Mass Destruction Civil Support Teams (WMD-CST):
The National Guard has established and certified WMD-CSTs capable of operating in a contaminated environment. The primary WMD-CST mission is to provide rapid agent identification, assessment, advice, and assistance to the local onscene/ incident commander.

▪ Interim Evaluation:
CONSEQUENCE MANAGEMENT VERSION 1.0

Please select the response to the following statements that is closest to your opinion.

Consequence Management Version 1.0 familiarizes CCMRF battalion and brigade level staff to their mission, roles, and responsibilities.

Yes
Yes, but (please explain reservation):
_____

No

Consequence Management Version 1.0 contextualizes existing doctrinal guidance to facilitate effective application of doctrine, strategy, and commander's intent when CCMRF elements face novel problems in the field.

Yes
Yes, but (please explain reservation):
_____

No

Consequence Management Version 1.0 provides senior operational staff with a ready reference to inform decisions during exercises and when deployed.

Yes
Yes, but (please explain reservation):
_____

No

Consequence Management Version 1.0 provides the civilian counterparts of the CCMRF operational staff with information to facilitate their effective collaboration with the CCMRF.

Yes
Yes, but (please explain reservation):
_____

No

After reading Consequence Management Version 1.0 I understand the CCMRF's mission, roles and responsibilities and the core principles behind doctrine, strategy, and commander's intent and am ready to apply those principles when facing a tactical decision not specifically anticipated in training or when C3 capabilities have been compromised.

Yes
Yes, but (please explain reservation):

_____

No

In the next version of Consequence Management I would like to have:

_____
_____
_____
_____
_____
_____
_____
_____
_____
_____
_____
_____
_____
_____
_____
_____

Made in the USA
Monee, IL
06 January 2023

24683580R00115